SCENES IN THE SOUTH,

AND OTHER

MISCELLANEOUS PIECES,

BY THE LATE

COL. JAMES R. CREECY.

WASHINGTON:
THOMAS McGILL, PRINTER.
1860.

DEDICATED

TO OUR GIFTED FRIEND,

MRS. MARY STANFORD,

OF NEW ORLEANS,

FORMERLY

MRS. COL. OSMAN CLAIBORNE,

OF MISSISSIPPI.

CONTENTS.

MISCELLANEOUS;

INTRODUCTION.

Immediately after the decease of my husband, Col. James R. Creecy, I anticipated having published a work of magnitude and value, written by him at the express desire of several members and senators, portraying the manners, customs, habits, and plantation life in the south. The MSS., to my great disappointment, and still greater pecuniary loss, was mislaid in the publishers' hands in New York, the more to be regretted from its having been written expressly for the press, and much time and talent expended on it.

The present work I have now compiled, is composed of fugitive pieces, loose MSS. found in a port-folio, and consisting of matter which will be well-calculated to amuse some, instruct others, and sincerely do I hope interest all *who have been so kind as to give their influence in the publication of Scenes in the South!*

SCENES IN THE SOUTH.

THE FATHER OF WATERS.

ON the morning of a lovely day in October, in 1834, I first saw the mouth of the Father of Waters; and the wildness and desolation of the scene will ever remain deeply engraved on my memory. I was a passenger in a fine new ship of over five hundred tons, and had enjoyed a most delightful trip of six days from the Chesapeake. A pilot had boarded us the evening before, and as we approached the Balize, my first *impression* was the vast extent of marsh: so waste, so uninhabitable, so lonely, so like the Great Desert of Sahara, in monotony and dreamy stillness!—a dreary home for alligators, mud-turtles, cat-fish, and sea birds! The *view* produced a melancholy sensation at my heart, which I could not easily get rid of. And now the steam-tug came out, puffing and snorting to shame the hordes of wild horses of the Western Prairies; tearing up the muddy waters, which extend miles into the deep blue Gulf, apparently determined to take possession of Neptune's briny empire, *by force*, positively refusing its offered amalgamating embraces, and standing aloof, walled up, marking distinctly the line of march!

We were hailed, boarded, and soon taken in tow by the foremost boat, and jerked rapidly into the swift current of the Mississippi, where, for miles on both sides of the channel way, on entering, were piled, in wild confusion, thousands of trunks, bodies, and the larger limbs of trees, bereft of foliage and bark; bleached till white as human bones on the fields of Waterloo, and looking like the skeletons of departed glories, once the majestic beauty and pride of the river in higher regions, thousands of miles away north. We were anchored just above the light-house at the S. W. Pass, and away our tug dashed and puffed for other *tows* now in sight, bound in. We luxuriated on choice fish and oysters, purchased from boats soon along side, for the oysters of that region are equal in flavor to any in the world, and the fish only inferior to the hog fish of Lynn Haven Bay. About 10 P. M. our tug came along, with a brig astern and a ship on one side, grappled us to the other, and bounded away at the rate of eight miles per hour, against a four-mile current, for the Crescent City; and, malgre all stoppages and necessary delays, we were safely secured before 1 P. M. the next day at a wharf nearly in front of the United States Mint. With what astonishment did I, for the first time, view the magnificent levee, from one point or horn of the beauteous crescent to the other, covered with active human beings of all nations and colors, and boxes, bales, bags, hogsheads, pipes, barrels, kegs of goods, wares and merchandise from all ends of the earth! Thousands of bales of cotton, tierces of sugar, molasses; quantities of flour, pork, lard, grain and other provisions; leads, furs, &c., from the rich and extensive rivers above; and the wharves lined for miles with ships, steamers, flat-boats, arks, &c., *four deep!* The business appearance of this city is not surpassed by any other in the wide world: it might be likened to a huge bee-hive, where no drones could find a resting place. I stepped on shore, and my first exclamation was, "This is the place for a business man!" How many like me have said the same! How many such have there found early graves! How many have sickened and suffered deep and agonizing disappointment! And how many of the vast number of annual adventurers have ever realized their brilliant expectations and hopes!

THE CREOLES OF LOUISIANA.

THAT there is much *liberality*, *generosity*, *friendship*, and *kindness* in New Orleans cannot be questioned; but there is also a picayune disposition, a closeness of calculation, a savingness of manner indulged in by a large majority of the Creole population, that would teach a Yankee tin peddler lessons in economy. The Creoles generally live on less and make a display with less than can any Connecticut graduate of a savings college or school of onion raisers or straw braiders. They can do more with a bottle of poor claret, smiles, bows, shrugs, and grimaces, than a Virginian *of the first family* can with a dozen superior sparkling champagne worth twenty dollars. Politeness costs them nothing; smiles and bows are abundant and cheap, and in those commodities they are profuse and liberal. There is but little sterling, honest friendship in existence; and exhibition, outward show, and pretension are the ruling passions! A poor fellow, who lived on the coast adjoining the estate of a wealthy Creole planter, was met on foot, much fatigued, by the *Proprietaire*, who thus addressed him:

"Bon jour, mon ami. Mon Dieu! You appear ver moosh fatigue. Vat is mattair vis you?"

"Why, sir, I am just from court, which I was compelled to attend as a witness; the weather is warm, and 'tis a long walk for an old man."

"Ah, ha, you valk? Le diable! For vy you valk?"

"Because I have no horse to ride, sir."

"Mon Dieu! mon ami, mon voisin, you know J'ai nombres des chevaux—I have plenty horses; pourquois you don't send to me for a horse ven you valk such long vay; ha, my friend, my neighbor? Is too bad for you valk dare; you go anozair temps, you sen for my horse, certainment."

"Oh, I thank you most kindly, sir," replied *Lazarus*, who really supposed him in earnest; and the very next time he was compelled to attend court, he was green enough to send his son to borrow a horse from his rich *voisin*, when *Dives* responded with a choleric shrug:

"Mon Dieu! Dat man is dem fool! I not, no, *nevair*, lend my horse to nobody, be gar! I tell him so for de *compliment;* he no onderstan *de compliment;* go, tell your fardair, I not let to him my horse—dare—dat's de ting. I no lend my horse to nobody—dare!"

I do not wish to be understood as including the whole Creole population as having this littleness of soul, this low-lived Yankee peddling meanness. By no means: for I know there are many noble, princely exceptions.

Good claret is really good; but bad, is like unto Jeremiah's figs—the good are very good; the bad too bad to give the pigs! A few days after my introduction to a French Creole, of dashing exterior and dancing-master-like manners, I accidentally passed his residence on Rampart street, He was on the steps, recognized me, and after a profusion of bows and smiles, in sisted on my taking some wine with him; I consented, walked in, and the flourishes commenced. He rang a hand-bell violently. After some delay a servant girl made her appearance, and my host addressed her pompously:

"Adele! apportez instamment une bouteille de vin, bon et frais. Entendez? Vitement, vite!"

The domestique disappeared, and then compliments were thrown on me broadcast. Time passed, perhaps fifteen or twenty minutes, not quite long enough to manufacture the wine, but long enough to send to a grocer and have a bottle entered on the pass-book. At length Adele returned, *wind-broken*, with the precious liquid—but "*no long cork*," hermetically sealed, was to be drawn with the enlivening pop. It was a common black *junk* bottle, with a greasy *atom* of cork three-fourths of an inch in length, which was fingered from its new home, and with an additional flourish or two, the thin watery preparation, resembling, in flavor and color, a miserable mixture of vinegar and water stained with pokeberry juice, was decanted—bows, shrugs, and grimaces *encore*—when I swallowed a gill or so to the "votre sante" of my entertainer—may the Lord in his mercy forgive me!—and then, with a smile on my lips and a twinge in my heart, I took leave of my hospitable host forever.

LANGUAGES, DANCES, ETC., IN NEW ORLEANS.

THE Creoles of Louisiana are generally a gay, gallant, gaudy, graceful, sunny set, who can distance the cutest Yankee of all New England in economy any day in the year! In New Orleans, men from every State in the Union; from every country in North and South America; from every nation of Europe, and many from Asia and Africa, are to be found; and all business men who expect to succeed should speak at least three modern languages.

In a room where were assembled sixteen persons, I have heard four different languages spoken at the same time. *All talk!* One speaks

French, and is replied to in English. Another speaks German, and is replied to in Spanish. Another speaks Spanish, and is replied to in French, &c.—not one, at the time, conscious of or thinking of the language he uses! Many negroes speak three languages in such a manner as to defy you to tell which one of the three is their vernacular! New Orleans is the heaven of negroes, and in that city they are the happiest human beings that ever breathed the breath of life. They never know nor feel the sufferings of cold or hunger; and they are not obliged or compelled to *labor hard at any time* to procure food, clothing, and shelter. The diseases so fatal to strangers they are in a great measure exempt from; and altogether they are, beyond doubt, the most comfortable and joyous of God's creatures. There are many free negroes in the city and state; some of them wealthy and the owners of numerous slaves; and, strange as true, they are genenerally the *hardest* masters and mistresses.

North of Rampart street, about its center, is

the celebrated Congo Square, well enclosed, containing five or six or perhaps more acres, well shaded, with graveled walks and beautiful grass plats, devoted on Sunday afternoons to negro dances and amusements. The Creoles of Louisiana—Spanish, French and negroes—are Catholics, with but few exceptions, and on Sabbath mornings the females and a few elderly males are punctual in attending their religious duties. The holy mass is not neglected by those two classes, but the afternoons and evenings of the Lord's day are spent in amusements, fun, and frolic of every description—always with an eye to much sport for a little expense.

The "haut ton" attend operas, theaters, masquerades, &c. The quadroons have their dashing fancy balls, dances, &c.; and the lower order of colored people and negroes, bond and free, assemble in great numbers in Congo Square, on every Sunday afternoon in good weather, to enjoy themselves in their own peculiar manner. Groups of fifties and hundreds may be seen in different sections of the square, with banjos, tom-toms, violins, jawbones, triangles, and various other instruments from which harsh or dulcet sounds may be extracted; and a variety, indeed, of queer, grotesque, fantastic, strange, and merry dancers are to be seen, to amuse and astonish, interest and excite, the risibles and wonder of "outside barbarians," unskilled in Creole or African manners and customs.

Sometimes much grace and often surprising activity and long-continued rapid motions are seen. The dancers are most fancifully dressed, with fringes, ribbons, little bells, and shells and balls, jingling and flirting about the performer's legs and arms, who sing a second or counter to the music most sweetly; for all Africans have melody in their souls; and in all their movements, gyrations and attitudenizing exhibitions, the most perfect time is kept, making the beats with the feet, heads, or hands, or all, as correctly as a well-regulated metronome! Young and old join in the sport and dances. One will continue the rapid *jig* till nature is exhausted; then a fresh disciple leaps before him or her and "cuts out" the fatigued one, who sinks down gracefully on the grass, out of the way, and is fanned by an associate with one hand, while water or refreshments are tendered by the other.

When a dancer or danseuse surpasses expectation, or is particularly brilliant in the execution of "flings" and "flourishings" of limb and body, shouts, huzzas, and clapping of hands follow, and numerous *picallions* are thrown in the ring to the performers by (*strange*) spectators. All is hilarity, fun, and frolic. To witness such a scene is a certain cure for ennui, blue-devils, mopes, horrors, and dyspepsia. Hundreds of nurses, with children of all ages, attend, and many fathers and mothers, beaux and belles, are there to be found; there, where no cares or sorrows intrude; where pains and heart-aches are forgotten; where duns are unknown, and all earthly troubles cease to torment, *pro tem.* Every stranger should visit Congo Square when in its glory, once at least, and, my word for it, no one will ever regret or forget it. It is human nature to love to look on happy, joyous, smiling faces, and there no others are to be seen. The gaieties continue till sunset; and at the "gun-fire" the whole crowd disperse, disappear, and "the noise and confusion" in Congo Square is heard and seen no more until the next blessed Dimanche.

THE SONS OF ERIN IN THE CRESCENT CITY.

For many years the annual influx of the lowest order of Irish into New Orleans has been immense, and the numbers who are buried in the "swamp," subjects of yellow jack and cholera, are astonishing; and yet their places are instantly filled up, as are the ranks of well-disciplined troops in destructive battle. Eight out of ten who are attacked by those diseases become victims; and perhaps at least one-third of every importation have one or the other or both of those dreadful diseases. Nine-tenths of all the diseased poor immigrants who find shelter and attention in the numerous hospitals are foreigners, by far the greater number of whom are Irish of the lowest and worst character; reckless, abandoned, drunken, lying, dirty, ignorant wretches, who are more at home in the police office than anywhere else; and, as the fun-loving John Duggan would say, "Dthey ar' niver at pace until dthey ar' in a fight intirely!" Thousands of them leave every summer for the upper country, where they do not fare much better than in New Orleans. They are never employed except from necessity. The negroes have decidedly the preference, and readily obtain much higher wages. The Irish females are as disorderly and dissipated as the males, and 'tis sickening to see what numbers are every morning taken before the recorders for crimes and misdemeanors the preceding night! All laborers of good habits can obtain work and good pay in New Orleans. Living is not so dear as in this city, (Washington,) and beggars are seldom seen. But a few days after my arrival, I was standing at the corner of Royal and Canal streets with Dr. K——, when a stout, hearty, comfortably clad Irish woman interrupted our conversation by thrusting her hand between us, and saying, in the very richest brogue of Tipperary:

"Wud yer 'onners be plaised to give me a quarter iv a dollar?"

To get rid of her *speedily*, I handed her a "bit," and so did the Dr., who said:

"Why don't you go to work and earn money? You are strong enough for anything."

She *fobbed* the change, and with the most cunning look and roguish wink I ever witnessed, replied, as she turned away:

"*Who the divil d'ye think 'ud work*, when dthey can git a hoonderd dollars a moonth be beggin?"

CATHOLIC BURYING GROUNDS—ALL SAINTS' DAY.

THE first of November is indeed a memorable day in New Orleans, and on that day, in 1834, I first witnessed a scene which, for solemnity and pathetic effect on the finer feelings of the human heart, will never be surpassed. I was invited to accompany a family of friends to the Catholic burying grounds, and was told that I would be deeply interested in the exhibitions and ceremonies of the day, and would see a vast concourse of people, citizens and strangers, who annually attend to participate in or look upon the sacred right or custom never forgotten or neglected by the Creole population. I thought but little of my intended visit, or what I was to see or hear; but walked on, thinking and speaking of other things, until we arrived at the first gate to the resting-place of the departed, where sat a man jingling a dish or bowl containing silver change to attract the attention of *new comers.* All of our party contributed, and we entered the sacred grounds, when my astonishment was great indeed. Magnificent and costly tombs, vaults, and the humblest gravestones, were adorned, dressed, and decorated; some most richly, with costly materials—silks satins, muslins, and cloths. Beautiful and many-colored lamps were blazing in all directions and forms; lovely flowers in vases, pots, and jars; splendid bouquets and tasteful wreaths were entwined and interspersed, in various forms and figures, over all the quiet dead. No fėstive mirth was there; no gay and sprightly laugh was heard; no merry smile was seen; no prattling wit, no mirthful thought, no joyous sound, had *place* in all that hushed and humbled assemblage. My heart melted, and my memory went back to my mother's grave, far, far away. For it had pleased high Heaven to cast my *lot* so, that to visit the last home of my infantile *love* and subsequent *veneration*, annually, was impossible.

Oh, how heavenly, holy, how dear and sweet, the melancholy sensation, to see, to know, that death had not obliterated from the living the memory of friends and kindred, though deeply buried "low in the ground!" How sweetly happy was I to see the silent tear of affection, still living, trickling down the cheek of the young and old, while bending with clasped hands in pure devotion over the sad remains of long-lost loved ones: the child thus remembering its parents—the parents their children—the brother his sister—the sister her brother—the husband his wife—the wife the husband and partner of her joys and sorrows and hopes! And still more, and as interesting, perhaps, to see *slaves* sobbing and mourning over the graves of their masters and mistresses, many prostrated, overcome with sorrow; and nurses weeping over the children of their owners, who had died in their arms, after months and years of attention and kindness and love; the memory retaining a warm place in their honest hearts, and calling forth, year after year, prayers and tears of affection and love. I have witnessed numerous instances of this divine feeling in the breasts of female slaves for the children of their masters entrusted to their care; I have seen them grieve when the name of a deceased child was mentioned, long, long after its father had ceased to drop a tear to its memory.

That is the pure love from heaven—holy nature's love! Long may it live! We passed through cemetery after cemetery, (for there are three ancient ones, on a line, in the rear of Rampart street.) All were dressed, beautifully adorned, with festoons and fringes, and with all the charms of nature and art, in the richest manner, or most simply and neatly, as the means were had for one or the other. The light continued to burn the live-long night, and many of the devotees never left their places of mourning, where slept the mouldering and decayed remains of loved ones, long gone, till the dawn of another day reminded them of worldly duties to the living.

How hallowed, how heart-softening, how sweet, how heavenly, is this most affecting custom! Until I then witnessed it, I was ignorant of the existence of such an impressive and endearing ceremony in any country. How consoling must be the thought on the bed of death to know that once, at least, each passing year, some friend or relative will certainly visit, ornament, and drop a tear of fond and tender recollection on your grave! remember your virtues; your faults forgiven, forgotten! How sweet, when we must die, to know there lives even *one* kind friend who will bend in prayer over our earthly remains, and remember us kindly at least once a year! I had a dearly loved, gallant son, laid "low in the ground," in the bright bloom of youthful manhood, some months after my departure, perhaps *forever*. A year or more had elapsed, my heart still throbbing with grief for his premature exodus, when I received a letter from an angelic girl who knew him, telling me, in the purity of her soul, that, on her return from a summer trip north, she had visited my poor boy's grave and dropped a tear, with a wreath of flowers, on it, in the name of friendship for me and mine. A few more months *only* passed away, ere the God of Heaven, (in His wisdom,) who gives and takes, called that dear, sweet, "angelic girl" to His home of glory and happiness on high, (for she was too good for this world,) and her remains now rest not far from his for whom she wept, to receive the annual tear-drop from many a friend who will never forget her worth and beauty.

This custom is a heartfelt, pure, and heavenly one, that does honor to the Creole population of the Crescent city, and might be adopted by all religious denominations, without a charge or suspicion of bigotry or sectarianism, as evidence of living charity, love, friendship, and endearing recollection of deceased associates, too often *too soon* forgotten.

MILITARY PARADES IN NEW ORLEANS.

All Creole families who have a rood of ground or more, cultivate and sell more or less flowers and fruits. The most beautiful and finest peaches in the world are produced in Louisiana and Mississippi; but apples and cherries do not thrive well. Melons of delicious flavor and the largest size grow in those States. I have seen watermelons often weighing from forty to sixty pounds. Please say why do poor people live in a cold country?

The military parades of the Creole volunteers take place on the Sabbath; and the "Place d'Armes," a square immediately in front of the old Spanish Cathedral, is the muster-ground;

and while the organ in the venerable edifice is pealing anthems to HIM on high, while the holy mass is being presented to the pious worshippers, the words of command, clash of arms, rolling of drums, the fife's shrill whistle, and the crack of rifles, are heard above all!

The public gambling houses, which were open at all hours and well attended, were suppressed or prohibited in 1836, I think. Whether any good has resulted from it is more than doubtful; for the gambling is carried on, perhaps, to as great an extent now, privately, and the victims and their robbers are only the more cautious, hypocritical, and deceitful. In the public establishments many young men were deterred from venturing or exposing themselves, and dared not indulge in the vice at all for fear of losing their situations, or not obtaining them, if in want; now, those who are cursed with the infernal propensity, ruinously enjoy it, sneakingly, in private. I have reflected deeply on this subject; and, as *people will gamble*, I think it would be better for wives, children, and friends if gambling houses were licensed and heavily taxed. The debased would then be more generally known, and the evil consequences of their misdeeds more readily guarded against.

The contrast in the customs, habits, and manners of the citizens or residents of the different municipalities is remarkable West of Canal street is the *American* part of the city, and there the Sabbath is respected as in a New England village. All the stores, drinking-houses, and places of business, theaters, &c., are closed; the churches are well attended, mornings, afternoons, and nights; and all the rowdy, vulgar, and dissipated sons of or from the northern, eastern, and western States, who desire to frolic on that day, leave that section of the city, and participate in the enjoyments of the Creole population, at horse-races. bull-fights, expeditions to the Lake, &c.

THE MARCHANDES OF NEW ORLEANS.

THE street pedlars in New Orleans are a queer set. The rabais carry a great variety of small and necessary articles (which are constantly used or wanted in every family) in a kind of *hand-barrow*, with a frame or box at each end, and straps resting on the shoulders, while the rabais is placed in the middle, holding each side with one hand. It has four posts or legs, about eighteen inches in length, on which it stands when the rabais stops to trade or rest. The weight must be sometimes seventy or eighty pounds. He wends his weary rounds from early morn to dewy eve, singing monotonously, but loudly,

"Rabelle a bais a bas!" "Rabelle a bais a bas!" constantly when without a customer. A fair translation of his cry I never could obtain, but it is perfectly understood, and all the little boys and girls, mammas and servants, hail his appearance as he trudges along, wearied, yet chanting all the while, from street to street, his unvaried "Rabelle a bais a bas!" till he is called, when, stopping, he sits on the off-side of his carryall, and begins his little *trafiquer*. The rabais are numerous, particularly in the French and Spanish parts of the city; but they faithfully and religiously observe and keep sacred the holy Sabbath, which no other traders or laborers or artisans do in these quarters. The magazines in the first and third municipalities are all open; carpenters, masons, blacksmiths, painters, &c., are all at work; drays are rattling through the streets; cafés are open and thronged; balls, theaters, operas, and masquerades are in full operation and well attended, on the evening of the day proclaimed in the

Decalogue, as one of rest and peace and prayer.

The Creole slaves perform a harder duty on that holy day than on any other in the week. The scouring, washing, and cleaning is done on that day generally. Many of the female slaves are *marchandes* during the week, and their shrill cries never cease from morning's dawn till *"le milieu de la nuit"—Marchande de tait; marchande des pâtés, tous chauds;* marchande des oranges, douces tres douces; marchande des ooufs, Creoles, *tous frais;* marchande des galettes chauffe; marchande des plants; marchande des figues, douces et frais, and marchandes in everything to eat and drink or use in a *small way,* for the Creoles buy everything in that way. When a Creole gives a dinner party, the cook purchases and brings on her shoulders from the marchande de bois a picallion's worth of wood *pour l'occasion!*

THE BOUQUETIERS.

The bouquetièrs are an interesting and joyous class of marchandes, and a most beautiful and splendid exhibition they ever make. Numbers of them are to be seen daily and nightly at all the public places, and at the corners of the most frequented streets, nearly all of them neatly and prettily attired—the ever fashionable *madrass* tastily arranged as a head-dress or turban. They are generally quadroons or mulattoes, of handsome appearance, petite figures, with sparkling black eyes, beautiful teeth, and pleasing manners, and they have such a finished tact at disposing of their fragrant and splendid bouquets, that a stranger is fortunate, indeed, who can escape their entreaties and inducements to buy at whatever price they may demand; the smiles and courtesies are ever ready, and the sweetly uttered—

"Je vous remercie, monsieur," on exchanging a bouquet for a piastre, almost tempts one to buy another.

The wily bouquetière sees the effect of her *costume*, and plays off her skill again with almost certain success, in this way—

"Voulez vous un autre, monsieur, *pour madame*? Voici, voila," holding up a beauty, "pour votre fille? Pour votre amitie? C'est tres joli—deux piastres, simplement; achetez, monsieur? Oh! merci, merci, monsieur; *Je vous remercie*," taking the two dollars and handing over the bouquet with looks, and smiles, and wiles worth two more at least.

The most lovely flowers and ornamental shrubs are there ever in bloom and verdure; and there is no difficulty whatever in procuring magnificent bouquets any month in the year. Native and exotic plants and flowers of the richest description are cultivated and reared to perfection in the open air; and the trade in flowers, &c., is one of considerable magnitude.

MARDIGRAS.

Shrove Tuesday is a day to be remembered by strangers in New Orleans, for that is the day for fun, frolic, and comic masquerading. All the *mischief* of the city is "alive and wide awake," and in active operation. Men and boys, women and girls, bond and free, white and black, yellow and brown, exert themselves to invent and appear in grotesque, quizzical, diabolical, horrible, humorous, strange, masks and disguises. Human bodies are seen with heads of beasts and birds; beasts and birds with human heads; demi-beasts, demi-fishes; snakes' heads and bodies with arms of apes; man-bats from the moon; mermaids, satyrs, beggars, monks, and robbers, parade and march on foot, on horseback, in wagons, carts, coaches, cars, &c., in rich confusion, up and down the streets, wildly shouting, singing, laughing, drumming, fiddling, fifeing, and *all throwing flour broadcast* as they wend their reckless way, regardless of the recipients' comfort, and careless of their eyes or clothes; laughing loudly at threatened punishment, and adroitly escaping all attempts at redress. Thus they ride and run, and dash and flash, and fling their flour about, to the delight, amusement, and astonishment of the great mass of spectators, malgre the liberal donations of hands full of *flour* constantly applied, right and left, which in clouds fall upon those within reach; for all the fraternity carry their pockets full. One large *nondescript* car (drawn by four horses, uniquely caparisoned and *draped* with fiery dragons, serpents with numerous heads, scorpions with many stinging tails, &c.,) was the moving prison of his most satanic majesty, ignominiously and vulgarly *chained securely*—head, horns, tails, and all—blowing from his volcanic mouth, flames of fire and fumes of sulphur, surrounded with his familiars, imps of the most infernal appearance conceivable, "cutting up" and playing antics that would astonish Macbeth's witch and her cauldron attendants; whooping, yelling, groaning, grinning, and gibbering in such a manner as to occasion doubts in spectators whether they should laugh or cry, be amused or frightened. This carnival is permitted by the city authorities, sometimes rather reluctantly, and has been more than once forbidden, as well as the Congo Square dances; but the Creole propensity for those amusements is so strong that their friends are soon placed in power again, and the wild frolics are hailed by acclamation, as the masquers and fun and mischief-loving revelers make their appearance. This is the last day of enjoyment before the commencement of Lent, and it is a custom to which the old citizens were, and their descendants are, much attached, and it will be difficult to prevent its continuance. Upon the whole, there is much more amusement than positive evil in it, and it is as well, perhaps, to let it alone.

THE CHARIVARI IN NEW ORLEANS.

THE *charivari* is another extraordinary custom, in some respects peculiar to New Orleans, which is indulged in, generally, when an odd, unequal, or *uneven* pair is *married*—as a very young man to an elderly woman, or *au contraire;* or when a very rich man marries a very poor girl, or *au contraire;* or when a fine-looking man marries a hard-featured woman, who is very wealthy, and is blessed with *carroty* locks, cross-eyes, freckled skin, *turnip* nose, teeth like a roughly-used garden rake, and suspected of an evil tongue and a *Caudle* temper; or when a man or woman of doubtful or questionable blood marries one whose blood is thought to be pure and unmixed, or when old bachelors and maidens, far in the sear and yellow leaf, unexpectedly become Hymen's victims. Then, immediately upon the knowledge of any such event, Captain RICARDO, for years the head, heart, and spirit of the celebrated "Sheet Iron Band," issues his proclamation; and, as the 9 o'clock P. M. gun fires, blows his horn, when, as if by magic, his well trained, noisy troops assemble by hundreds at the spot designated, obedient to orders. Old Rick addresses them briefly; and, not being a member of Congress, he only speaks of the subject and object of the meeting—never flies the track to abuse and insult his associates, or make personal explanations, or new Presidents. No, indeed; Ricardo is a man of business; he does what he ought to do, only, and directs his command to do the same, and they do it. Their heterogeneous collection of musical and noisy instruments are put in order, and away they march to the happy home of the newly married couple. Their arrival is announced by soft and gentle music, "Home, sweet home;" "Wooed, an' married, an' a';" "Sweetly ring the marriage *bells;*" And *then* old Rick *rings the bell*, politely requests an interview with the enchanted groom, and respectfully asks of him a donation, in consequence of his happy turn of fortune, of one, two, four, five hundred, or a thousand dollars, (as the circumstances may justify,) for the benefit of the "Female Orphan Asylum!" As the custom is well known and understood, the *first* request is generally complied with; when the company, with much good feeling, serenade the bridal party sweetly, ending with "The bairns ar' nae at hame yet." But sometimes the uxorious debutant is provoked at such an interruption of his early "honey moon," and has the temerity to *refuse*. Rick never presses his claim *courteously twice* the same night; no, he blandly bows himself out, and at a signal the whole "Sheet Iron Band" sounds the "alarum of refusal!" And then such a din, such "noise and confusion," such rattling of dry bones, blowing of horns and conchs, sounding of gongs and trumpets and rattles, and beating of drums, salute the *cooing doves*, that "tired nature's sweet restorer, balmy sleep," visits no disciple of the drowsy god, in that house or that neighborhood, till the next matin bells do ring for early devotees. Some few obstinate and miserly "*hindiwiduals*" hold out and keep their purses tight and close, but Ricardo and his band attend him as regularly as the booming of the gun, or the vesper hymn, and he now demands (for he requests but once) generally double the amount first asked. The wild and screeching, thundering serenade is continued night after night until the worn down victim of an unequal marriage either runs away, "slopes for Texas," or parts unknown—wife, money, and all—or pays the demand; which is, certainly, the very next day *faithfully* delivered to the superintendent of the asylum, and the amount received is faithfully chronicled in the city papers. Many thousands of dollars have been added to this most charitable institution by the exertions and eccentricities of the amiable, kind, and good-hearted Ricardo.

NATCHEZ.

Early in December, 1834, I landed at Natchez, having made the trip from New Orleans *in rather less than three days*—a brag passage at that time. I was comfortably quartered at Parker's Hotel, and was detained there by business several weeks.

Natchez "*under the hill*" was then the terror of all decent and moral people; crimes of the deepest dye were reported as being committed daily and nightly. Gambling, drunkenness, and beastialities of the most infernal description were known to be perpetrated, but generally under such circumstances that the laws of the land could not reach the guilty, and Lynch law was often resorted to by some of the very best citizens, to punish those who could not be punished in any other way. Whether the excuse was entirely sufficient I leave to those better skilled in laws divine and human. "*Necessitas non habet leges.*"

A man named Foster was then in prison for murdering his wife under circumstances of the grossest brutality, and, as was understood and believed, without a shadow of cause or provocation. He was, if not wealthy, at least perfectly independent, for his property was valued at twenty thousand dollars, clear of debt. He had been in prison for some months, and by some queer or strange law then in force in Mississippi, no man could be tried for any offence, if *a* court or *two* (I do not recollect the particulars perfectly) were suffered to pass during his imprisonment without *his being brought to trial*, and by some quirk or quibble of his counsel, this happened in the case of Foster. It was known that *under that law*, at the approaching session of the court, the judge would be compelled to discharge *Foster;* turn him loose upon an outraged community, unscathed, unwhipped of justice, his hands reeking with the blood of his virtuous and butchered wife, to exult and gloat over his infamy, and, like a wild beast *once* fed on human flesh and blood, acquiring an insatiable love for such food, to hunt for other victims.

The best part of the community became excited. It was *whispered* that he should not so escape. When the court met and the judge was applied to by Foster's counsel to discharge him as the law directed, he was taken from the jail to the court-house by the sheriff, accompanied by some two hundred or more citizens of Natchez, among them many of the most respectable, wealthy, and worthy. The judge, upon hearing the fate of the case and reading the law aloud as applicable, formally dismissed or discharged him. The sheriff walked with him to the door, when, without "noise or confusion," a *committee* of the citizens assembled, *invited* him to take a walk! The liberated criminal, as pale as a corpse, understood instantly the object of the invitation, and saw that *opposition* would be useless; two gentlemen seized him, each by a shoulder, a line was formed almost in silence, and the word "*march*" was pronounced finally by a tall man in front. The whole crowd moved as regularly as a well-trained regiment. No shouts, no threats, no exhibition of passion were heard or seen. He was taken quietly to the suburbs of the city, stripped, whipped most severely, tarred and feathered, and then marched back into the city, with a fife and drum playing the "rogue's march." It was nearly sunset when the Lynchers and their victim neared the jail; some such exclamations were heard as "Take him to the river, tie him to a log, and set him adrift." "Hang the villain, who more richly deserves the gallows." "Never turn such a fellow loose to butcher another wife." A lawyer of some celebrity, S. M. Grayson, (since dead,) at that moment jumped on the steps of the jail, pulled off his hat, and said with a loud voice: "My friends, we have *done* our duty as good citizens, and I now propose that we all go quietly to our homes!" But little if any objection was made; and in that short time the sheriff skillfully managed to get Foster into the jail and locked the door, securing him from the multitude for the moment at least. I saw him for the first time, as he was assisted or rather forced up the steps; and he was the *first* victim to Lynch law I had ever seen! Almighty Father, what a picture! He was more like a huge shapeless fowl, covered with masses of feathers, all turned the wrong way, than anything else. He had been severely lacerated, thoroughly coated with tar, and a large bag of feathers were glued to his person, from the crown of his head to the soles of his feet! That night, *late*, his friends (for a man worth twenty thousand dollars will have friends) took him secretly from the jail, and I never heard from him afterwards.

LYNCH LAW IN NATCHEZ.

An Italian was found secreted in a store late at night—no door or window had been broken, nothing belonging to the premises was found upon his person. He refused explanations, and would answer no questions whatever. He was taken before the authorities, very strongly suspected of evil design, as the store but a few nights previous had been robbed of rich goods to a large amount. Nothing could be proved against him, except his being in the store, and he was discharged. Instantly he was walked off by a crowd of citizens to where a gallows had been erected some time previous, a few hundred yards south of the city. I almost involuntarily *followed*, and with a beating heart expected to see the poor devil hung outright. He was taken under the gallows, stripped, tied down securely, and the lash applied most powerfully to his back and shoulders till fifty blows were counted, when a cessation took place, and the question was put to him:

"Who are your accomplices, and where are the stolen goods?"

Up to this moment he had not spoken a word or exhibited any feeling; and then his simple reply was:

"Kill a me!"

Fifty more stripes were repeated, and this game was continued until the miserable devil received *five hundred lashes!* He spoke no other word during the whole time, but replied audibly to each question, "Kill a me." He survived the punishment—arose from the ground after being untied, with the assistance of one of his countrymen, (who was strongly suspected of being one of his associates in robbing the store,) walked into the city, and I never more heard of them.

Now, I am unwilling to be thought an advocate of Lynch law, for I have a natural aversion to violence and outrage, and am opposed entirely to *capital punishment* for any crime. I cannot believe that *man* has any right to take away what he cannot restore, should be subsequently assertain that he had taken it unjustly. I believe that punishment should be inflicted on criminals; but I know that hanging a man is the very worst use a man can be put to. And I also believe, that when the laws of the land cannot reach a villain, evidently and palpably guilty of atrocious offences, I *might* look on the operation of Lynch law with some degree of composure, although I could not, would not aid and assist.

PORT GIBSON.

I ARRIVED at Port Gibson, rather a pretty little town on Bayou Pierre, a few miles from Grand Gulf, Mississippi, about sunset one evening, in the summer of 1835. Some court was in session, the public houses crowded, the musquitoes (a pestilence forgotten or unknown to the chronicles of Egyptian plagues) too blood-thirsty and numerous to mention, and to sleep without a "bar" or netting was, to a thin-skinned Anglo-Saxon, utterly impossible. So, I had my horse taken care of the moment after I dismounted, hunted for the landlord, who I happened to know, and inquired if he could furnish me with a bed, secured in such a manner that I might enjoy "tired nature's sweet restorer, balmy sleep." He said if I would "go to bed" immediately, he could give me one. It was then not fairly dark, but I said:

"Well, sir, I have ridden forty miles over a rough road to-day, am much tired, and I will retire so soon as you will show me a bed."

He took a candle and went with me to a room in the second story, where there were *three* tolerably decent beds, well protected against the buzzing vampires, *two* of which were already occupied.

"There," said he, "is a good bed, sir, take possession of it at *once*, or some other person will have it in less than ten minutes."

He left the room and shut the door. I took off my coat, vest, stock, &c., and was in the act of drawing off one of my boots with the aid of a chair, when a fellow apparently half drunk, with a cigar in his mouth, opened the door very rudely, and stepping within eight or ten feet of me, rather impertinently said:

"That's my bed, sir, and I mean to sleep in it."

"Not to-night, sir," said I.

"Who showed you that bed, sir," said he.

I replied very mildly—

"Mr. Reed, the landlord, sir."

"Do you know who I am, sir," said he.

"No, sir, nor do I care," said I, taking a firm hold of the chair with both hands; for I did not intend to give up my bed.

"Why, sir," said he, "I'm captain here!"

"Oh, ho!" said I, "you're *only* a captain, are you; very well, then, sir, I *out-rank* you entirely, for I am lieutenant-general and commander-in-chief of this division, and do you obey orders instantly. Right about face, and march directly out of this room," raising the chair at the moment, with a look that he could not misunderstand, when, to my astonishment, the scamp ran out of the door and burst out into a horse-laugh, where he was joined by three or four associates, who fairly shouted at his discomfiture; and I learned enough as they retired to satisfy me that it was a *ruse*, a dastardly attempt to get my bed by "bluffing me off the track," as was the expression.

The inmates of the other two beds were wonderfully amused at the way in which I got rid of the fellow; and really I was happy at the laughable termination, for I found myself more excited than I was aware of, as I most certainly should have tried the temperature of his head with the chair, if he had continued the game any longer.

The next morning, Mr. Reed mentioned that my interrupter had requested him to apologize and to introduce him to me. I refused, positively, any acquaintance or association with a man who would have deprived me of a bed, if he could have played upon my fears, and was willing to make me an object of contempt and ridicule for his tipsy companions. Such conduct is palpably wrong and *dangerous;* and as I never amused or indulged myself in any tricks of the kind, I could think of no excuse for others.

DANGERS OF SOUTHERN TRAVELERS.

A FEW days after, I was on my way to Jackson, and stopped at a house some seven or eight miles from the pleasant little town of Raymond, where I fared tolerably well, and left very early in the morning, so as to ride in the cool air, as was invariably my custom. Passing through a dense forest of low ground, about a mile in width, I met a man on foot with a heavy stick of unusual length in one hand. The sun was just rising, and as I approached him, he said, in a very respectful manner—

"I will speak to you a moment, if you please, sir."

I rode so near as to touch him with my left leg, and said meekly—

"What do you wish to say, sir?" looking him (rather searchingly) full in the eyes. He replied he had not a cent in the world; had been without a mouthful of food for twenty-four hours; was turned out of a house the evening before by some drunken fellows, who pretended he was distributing *abolition tracts*, and asked me to give him means to procure a breakfast.

I saw at once there was no evil design in the man, and I gave him a dollar, which happened to be convenient in my vest pocket, the smallest and all the change I had about me. He thanked me kindly, and requested to know my name and residence. I gave him the information asked for, and added, to his astonishment, this advice—

"That so long as he was in Mississippi, never to stop a stranger at such a time and in such a place again."

"Why, sir?" he startingly asked.

"Because," said I, "nine times out of ten you'll be shot if you do."

We parted, but we met once more, some years after, under different circumstances; which meeting I may give an account of before I close my "Scenes in the South."

On my arrival at Raymond, I mentioned my adventure at the breakfast table, when there was a unanimous opinion expressed by the whole number present *that they would have shot him!* I astonished all by saying with a smile—

"That had I been disposed to shoot him, I could not have done it, for I had never carried a weapon of any kind in my life!"

Just previous to that time, Phelps, the celebrated robber and murderer, was shot by the sheriff of Warren county at Vicksburg. He was condemned and sentenced to be hung; and on being taken out of prison for that purpose, had, with an iron bar to which his handcuffs were attached, bid defiance to the whole assembled multitude, and was steadily moving off, swearing he *would not be hung!* No entreaty had any effect on him, and most reluctantly the kind-hearted, humane, and generous sheriff, Stephen Howard, was, by his official obligations, compelled to shoot him. Thus died one terror of Mississippi! There were numerous robbers and gamblers, closely allied, at that time in that State. Murrell's gang had just been betrayed or exposed by Stewart; and nearly all persons went armed completely. I was almost a solitary example of exception, and I have never regretted it.

I went to Jackson, attended to my business, passed through Madison county to Yazoo, where, after witnessing several strange events, I left for Vicksburg, by land; again crossing Big Black, through Madison and Hinds, and after numerous adventures, during two days and nights, reached that city the day after the *five gamblers* were hung, and while they were yet suspended on the gallows. What a scene! and what terrific excitement did I witness.

A long and faithful history of that awful, but

absolutely necessary transaction was written by me—submitted to the inspection and revision of two most estimable gentlemen who were deeply interested—and published subsequently in the Natchez Courier. It was republished throughout the United States and months afterwards I found it *entire* in a London paper. If ever respectable men on the face of this earth had an excuse for committing wholesale murder, the citizens of Vicksburg had one. Murderers, robbers, gamblers, thieves, and incendiaries had congregated and associated in that place to the number of (supposed) one hundred and fifty. They had defied the laws of God and man; they had scouted at virtue, modesty, and decency; they went doubly armed, and murders or outrages were perpetrated daily and nightly, openly and brutally.

A female of respectability risked insult every time she dared venture into the streets, and redress was out of the question. If husband father, or brother, presumed to call one of them to account, the pistol or bowie-knife were instantly used with a disgusting bravado of certain security.

Many young men, and too many older ones, were seduced or enticed (to their shame and disgrace) into the haunts, "the hells," of the villains, and swindled, cheated, fleeced, robbed of their all. Those acts and deeds had continued "till forbearance ceased to be a virtue," and after various conciliatory means to prevail on them to leave the city had been tried and failed, more stringent ones were attempted, when Dr. Bodely, a most worthy and valuable young man, was shot dead at the door of the principal and most notorious gambling establishment.

It was on the fourth of July; the volunteer companies were on parade, and on hearing of the murder of Dr. B., the unequaled excitement was allayed by the hanging of the *only five* miserable and unfortunate wretches that were caught!

I am not "fond of blood and carnage;" but after a lapse of nearly seventeen years, I am yet of the opinion that the numerous, extraordinary, diabolical, and villainous outrages committed by the gamblers and their associates in Vicksburg, justified (*if any thing in the sight of God could justify such an act*) the citizens of that place in thus ridding themselves of a most intolerable pestilence and deadly nuisance. I am *naturally* opposed to intemperance in all things, and deserve no credit, perhaps, for my habits, for I have made no sacrifices to possess them; but I do conscientiously believe that gambling, drunkenness, gluttony, tobacco and opium chewing and smoking, are *useless*, and when indulged in long, ruinous to the health of the victims, expensive and destructive, and the worst evils that curse society.

TEMPERANCE MAN IN THE SOUTH.

THE recklessness of disposition caused by intoxication is, *alone*, without the generally horrible consequences, quite a sufficient inducement for the friends of temperate habits to exert themselves in favor of exterminating from decent society the poisonous fluids which so often lead to ruin when used to excess. I am not fanatical in my opposition to the *use* of liquors, but to the *abuse* I will not "give an inch;" and, in my opinion, the filthy, disgusting, deleterious, and expensive use of tobacco and opium is but little better. How a man, with saliva oozing constantly from his mouth, befouling his chin and bosom, spitting on all around him, or ejecting a cloud of pestiferous smoke, almost enough to suffocate decent persons in his vicinity, can dare presume to lecture another for taking a glass of wine, or a drink of brandy and water, is beyond my comprehension; for the latter can be done without offending, soiling, or disgusting your associates.

On my way to Vicksburg, in the summer of 1835, when the thermometer was ninety degrees, and no ice to cool the tepid and muddy water, after I had drank several glasses, still thirsty and almost sick, I walked into the bar-room and asked for some brandy; for, in my opinion, no addition whatever could make the water worse. I prepared a glass, and as I was in the act of raising it to my lips, a man, dressed in a suit of dingy black, with a bloated face, evidently a confirmed, long-established *rum-sucker*, stepped up to me, with an enormous quid of tobacco in his mouth, the bosom of his shirt literally covered with the saliva which was then dribbling from his mouth, from which was issuing a most fetid breath, and impertinently addressed me, an entire stranger:

"Well, sir, I should have thought better of you than to see you set such an example *in public.*"

I drank my unpalatable mixture, and looking at him as mildly as possible under the circumstances, replied:

"I may be wrong, sir, in drinking thus openly, as far as the example goes, and perhaps it would have been better to have done it *privately.*"

My remark was lost, or there was no spot on his face that could be more highly colored by a *blush*, and I continued:

"When a man feels it his duty to correct another for a bad habit, he should not exhibit, so palpably, the positive effect of a worse one in his own person."

I felt provoked, and led him gently, by the arm, in front of a mirror, and pointing to it, said:

"With such a *face* and such a *bosom*, a lecture on temperance comes from *you, sir*, with a bad grace. Perhaps, you understand me?"

He replied, "I am a minister of the Gospel, sir; and, surely, you did not mean to insult me?"

I was rather mortified and astonished, but felt the more disgust towards him, and said, rather bitterly—

"I beg your pardon, sir, and assure you, that but for your information, I never should have suspected *you* of being one of God's messengers on this earth," and bowing, I left him alone in his glory. He was evidently more than half-drunk before we reached Vicksburg, but he certainly did not set *a bad example, by drinking in public as I did!*

Poor D——— had, at last, one more horrible frolic, and died not long after, in Natchez. I happened to be at his death-bed, and witnessed the sure and fatal effects of intemperance. He was well known in Upper Mississippi, for utter recklessness when drunk, which, unfortunately, occurred too often.

Nothing has been more unaccountable to me, from my boyhood, than the most extraordinary propensity many persons have to indulge to excess in the use of intoxicating liquors.

Some of the greatest men of the age and country, with colossal minds and Chesterfieldian manners, have become the victims of intemperance, and have died, degraded and debased to the level of brutes! Men, whose gifts and acquirements might have enabled them to eclipse the brightest luminaries of the literary and scientific world, have drank themselves into insignificance and contempt, and have been buried unhonored!

The opium and tobacco chewers and smokers, are, indeed, but little *above* the intemperate imbibers of alcoholic liquors, and have no more reason or excuse for their disgusting, filthy, deleterious, and expensive indulgences.

The *ladies*, (God bless them and preserve them

forever!) the ladies should set their faces and raise their hands and voices against the use of tobacco as well as liquor. They can do more than temperance societies. The pure and holy ministers of Christ should set the example, and preach against the use of tobacco, and against *gluttony*, too, as well as liquor; and let me close this article by saying, most emphatically, that I look upon *gluttony* as the most *beastly* and inexcusable of all vices, and fully as injurious to health and happiness as any other.

"Be temperate in all things."

ANECDOTE OF TWO SOUTHERNERS.

I HAD but just left my *temperance lecturer*, when a noisy row attracted my attention towards the head of the boat, and curiosity led me that way. As I stepped out, I saw three men in the act of shoving a horse overboard. He was saddled and bridled, and had a pair of saddle-bags, well filled, secured to the saddle by the stirrups being drawn through the loops. There were no guards or railing, and the job was not difficult, for overboard the poor horse went, with a grand hip, hip, hurra! chorus. I looked on, perfectly astonished, heard the unfortunate owner of the horse abused—Heaven knows for what—and threatened that if he made a *fuss*, he would be thrown after the horse! Among the high-handed operators in the cruel and inexcusable act was a man named W. D——, well known to me, who was notorious for his recklessness when indulging in his too frequent drunken frolics; but, when sober, was a kind-hearted and honorable man. He had been talking to me in the most kind and friendly manner, some time before he commenced drinking, and told me he had a large amount of money with him; but he was then so very drunk that I thought it best not to say anything to him. The unfortunate man who owned the horse came to me, *crying;* said he was from the western part of Georgia; that all his money and all his clothes, except what he had on, were in his saddle-bags; that the horse and contents of the bags were all his earthly property; that he was on his way to Arkansas, where he had some relatives, and what to do he knew not. I was reflecting what to do or say to help the poor fellow, when W. D——, as drunk as he was, noticed him in conversation with me; and, staggering towards us, said to me—

"Send that d——d fool to bed, and tell him to be quiet and stop his blubbering, or by G—d, I'll have him thrown overboard to follow his horse."

The Georgian moved off instantly, and for several hours I heard no more of him. D—— reeled away to the cabin, tumbled in a berth, and I took a seat very near him. He soon dropped into a heavy sleep, and I believe his associates followed his example. D—— slept some time, and, on rousing up and seeing me, said:

"Hilloa, C——, what are you doing here!"

"I have been waiting for you to *wake up*," said I, "to give you a good scolding."

"What for?" he asked, apparently nearly sober.

"Why," said I, "have you no recollection of throwing a poor man's horse, saddle-bags, money, clothes, and all he had on earth, into the river?"

"Did I?" said he, rubbing his eyes and raising himself up, "Well, by G—d, I wonder I didn't throw *him* in, along with his *plunder!* Where is he? Go and find out how much he lost, and what he thinks his goat of a horse was worth. I had no idea of hurting him, but when I cursed him and his horse, the damned fool cried like a whipped schoolboy, and the boys and I shoved his horse overboard, just because he cried." He then handed me a large and well stuffed pocket-book, saying, "Pay him all you think, or all he says he has lost. You will find about eleven thousand dollars in that book. Satisfy the poor devil, and tell him to hush crying;" and then, as calm as a "summer's morn," laid down to sleep again.

I soon found the poor Georgian, who was still in tears.

"How much money did you have in your bag?" said I.

"Sixty-three dollars," he replied.

"How much were your clothes worth?"

He hesitated a little, and said, "May-be, about thirty dollars."

"What was your horse worth?"

"Well, I reckon," said he, "nigh upon seventy-five dollars."

"Then," said I, "will two hundred dollars make you whole, and satisfy you entirely?" He saw me open the pocket-book, and saw the bank notes, when a total change came over him.

"Oh, yes, sir-ree, bob-tail horse-fly," he fairly shouted, jumping up and knocking his heels together.

I handed him two one-hundred dollar bills, and told him who gave it to him. He took them, but further speech was denied him—he was dumb. I left him, and returned to D——, who was half dozing. When I told him what his frolic had cost him, he poured three or four terrible curses on the Georgian, and said:

"Is that all?" and, looking into his pocket-book, took a fifty-dollar note, and insisted that I should add that much more to the amount, and tell him, "Never to cry again; and that if he would return in the boat, and stop at Dr. C——'s plantation, he might get his horse again, as well as his '*plunder*.' "

I delivered the money and the message to the happiest man I had seen in many a day. We parted at Vicksburg, and I have never heard more of him.

HOSPITALITY OF FIRST SETTLERS—PANTHERS, ETC.

When I first reached what was called the "new purchase," in Mississippi—a very large tract of the best cotton land in the State—the settlers were "few and far between," and generally *poor squatters.* The harmless and inoffensive Choctaws were still there; and *living,* to travelers in those regions, was *rude* indeed. *Log cabins* afforded almost the only shelter; and, perhaps, in a whole day's ride through an open wilderness, you would not meet with more than two of those. The most miserable apologies for beds sufficed for the hardy pioneers, and the worst and simplest furniture was only to be seen. Seldom was a decent or educated female to be found; and the negro women were generally ignorant of house-work, for the first taken into that country were only accustomed to field labors. To one fresh from the comforts and luxuries of life in the Atlantic States, the change and contrast were awful.

But few, indeed, of the early settlers gave a thought to gardens or vegetables, and their food was coarse corn-meal bread, rusty pork, with wild game ocasionally, and sometimes what was, most slanderously, called coffee, without milk or cream, and often without sugar. In my journeys, if, perchance, towards nightfall, I espied a cabin, with a vine, shrub, or flower cultivated about it, I knew a female was *there*, and my heart would throb with joy, for I knew that such things always indicated a little better fare than usual. If no such evidence presented itself, gloom would settle upon me, and I would struggle hard to bear the sufferings I knew were awaiting me.

One evening, late in autumn, (after riding many miles without seeing a hut or human being,) while yet in the forest, and darkness becoming *visible*, I heard the barking of a dog, and then the lowing of a cow. A few minutes more brought to my view a cabin, for my horse pointed his ears and quickened his pace, as much delighted at the *barking* and *lowing* as myself. As I approached, I saw a woman milking a cow; and one calf, in a small pen, near. I knew not whether the woman was black or white, but I addressed her in a very respectful manner, and inquired for the road to some little *ideal* embryo city I had understood was in the neighborhood. She answered,

"You're in the road, now; don't you see the blazes in the trees?" without raising her head.

"How far is it?" said I.

"Nigh upon twelve miles," she replied.

"I cannot get there to-night; I could not follow the blazes through the forest, after dark," I said, half-musingly. "Who lives here?"

"I do," said she, "*sich livin' as tis.*"

"You are certainly not alone?" said I.

"No," she replied, "looking up at me from her milking for the first time.

I saw she was, or had been, a white woman, coarsely clad, and browned by exposure, till she was nearly as dark as a Choctaw squaw.

"My dear madam," said I, "could you give me shelter to-night, and furnish me with food for my horse; I am quite fatigued, and my horse more so. I will pay you liberally, and thank you, indeed, most kindly."

"*Well, I dunno,*" said she; "some mighty mean people pass here sometimes; but we haint got much to steal, and you don't look like you had so much badness in you. You can *light* and rest till Sam gets home; he went out to shoot some meat 'bout an hour ago, for we haint got *none* in the house, and I heard the crack of his rifle as I was comin' to the *cup-pen,*" (cowpen)

I thanked her, and gladly dismounted; led my horse to where I saw a pole on the ground, with a primitive bucket tied to one end, near a hole in the yard, in which was a good supply of very bad water; helped my horse bountifully, drank out of the same vessel myself, and went to the front door of the cabin, where I took a seat on a block of wood. My horse followed me, and no doubt was thinking as seriously of his fare for the coming night as I was. The weather was rather pleasant, *a little cool;* but with my saddle-blanket, a very large, old fashioned cloak and saddle-bags, I knew I could prepare a comfortable "lodging on cold ground," if under a shelter, for I had slept thus in a cane-brake, sheltered by their bushy tops, and on that score I cared but little. I had learned to *fast* for twenty-four hours without the least inconvenience, but my horse had not learned any such lesson; and he told me, as plainly as a horse could tell me, he wanted his supper.

At that moment a shout was heard, and my *landlady*, who was in the cabin, exclaimed, joyfully,

"There's Sam, and I know he's got *meat*, for he never *hollers* when he *haint* got none."

Sam soon made his appearance; a stout, hardy, weather-beaten young man, and threw down the hind quarter of a fine, fat deer, carelessly wrapped up in the skin.

"There's the *idee*," said he, "first-rate and a quarter over; that's the way to tell it. Hilloa! how de do, stranger?" offering me his brawny hand in the kindest manner, which I shook with hearty good will, requesting his permission to remain during the night.

"Sartin, shure," he replied; "never refuse a bite or a part of my cabin to a stranger, so long as he is civil. I'll take care of your horse; I've got plenty of corn, fodder, and *pumpkins*."

I followed him, with my horse, to where a trough, rude and rough enough, was resting on two strong wooden forks, firmly driven in the ground, to one of which, with the halter, I secured my horse; and then, Sam taking a basket, we went in a small field adjoining, where, with the yet existing twilight, we gathered about twenty ears of Indian corn, perfectly dry and hard. Sam shouldered a pumpkin of goodly size, returned to the trough, where, after breaking the pumpkin into numerous pieces, they, with the corn, were placed in the trough, to the great delight of my hungry horse, who was a Tennessean, and quite up to corn and pumpkins. Sam dissappeared while I was congratulating the horse on his bright prospects, but in a few minutes returned with three large bundles of corn fodder, (corn blades cured in the sun,) which he threw down near enough, saying—

"There, old hoss, is a chance to feed for one night; help yourself, and go ahead, steamboat." Then, turning to me, said, "Come in, stranger, your hoss will do."

We walked towards the cabin, and, seeing his wife, said—

"Sally, spread yourself, gal, and see what you can do towards supper; I'm as hungry as a panther, and I reckon this stranger aint much better off."

"I'm *about; allers on hand*," said Sally, who had already a rousing fire; had cut at least four pounds of the venison into beautiful slices, and was on her way for water.

She soon returned, and I was delighted to see how carefully she washed, salted, and laid it on a clean wooden tray to drain. She then took from a keg about a half gallon of meal, sifted it, poured boiling water on it, threw in a little salt, made it up into small pones, wrapping each very carefully in the inner shucks of corn, fresh from the ear, scraped away the embers from one corner of the ample fire-place, laid them down and covered them over deeply, with hot ashes and embers. In a few minutes the lid of an old pine chest was decently prepared as a table—three plates, three pint bowls, *clean*, but a little cracked, and good, strong knives and forks. The venison was then quickly and artistically broiled, on an old (but *clean*) gridiron that had seen trouble, then left near the fire to keep warm in a deep plate; and in a very short time the corn cakes were drawn from the ashes and unrolled—done to a turn—the bowls were filled with milk, and all of this was accomplished speedily, without "noise or confusion." We drew our stools as near the chest as our knees would permit, and the *havoc* commenced. The venison was fat, juicy, and tender, the bread was sweet and good, and the milk above suspicion, "pure as the snow on the mountain's brow." There was a meal that Heliogabalus never dreamed of! And I now affirm that no Roman epicure of them all ever enjoyed a luxury (at whatever expense it was procured) more acutely than our humble but happy trio did this rich but simple *petite souper.* I was really happy, and "courageous and refreshed for future toil," and praised Sally's cooking "very extensively;" to which, *malgre* my temperate habits, I did ample justice indeed. I congratulated Sam on the possession of such a valuable wife, and made them both feel quite contented with themselves. About nine o'clock I walked out to see if my horse was as much pleased with his supper as I was with mine, and found the happy fellow still luxuriating on his pumpkins and corn!

The moon was up, clear and bright. The sky, the stars, the forest, and all of heaven's creation then in view was the picture of beauty, tranquillity, and happiness. Nothing could have looked more serene and lovely since Eden's early bloom.

I returned to the cabin, and heard a debating about my lodging. *Sam and Sally* had both resolved that I should occupy their only bed, but I firmly opposed it, and prepared my pallet, *instanter*, myself, which settled the difficulty.

I took off my boots, coat, vest and stock, and "laid me down to sleep." My worthy entertainers were quickly in bed and snoring, as none but laborers or gourmands can snore. In defiance of the unmusical concert, fatigue weighed down my eyelids, and I, too, slept.

About two o'clock, (the moon was high and brilliant,) a *scream*, such as I had never heard before, more like a female in the death-struggle from sudden violence than anything else I could imagine,, yet loud, shrill, and strong, startled all three of us to our feet. The fire yet gave some light, and in an instant Sam had his rifle and was wide awake. I had heard the Indian war-whoop, but I knew the Choctaws in that country were harmless and peaceable, and I inquired what noise that possibly could be.

"Why, it's a *tarnal* panther, and nothing shorter," said Sam, "after my calf."

And then, opening the door cautiously, he stepped out. I followed him, and found my horse, terribly alarmed, near the door. He had broken loose, or rather torn up the fork to which I had fastened him, and was trembling from his head to his feet. The cow came running towards us, perfectly frantic. We heard the calf bleat, and the crack of Sam's rifle was almost simultaneous. Without moving, he commenced reloading. I saw the panther bound over the fence into the road, halt, and look back, and before I thought Sam was ready, the dreadful beast had the second ball. He sprang at least his length from the ground and fell. Sam did not move, but again began to load his good rifle. I stepped towards the fence, thinking the panther was dead. Sam shouted out, "Stop," and came towards me, ramming down the bullet. We then walked quite near the fence, which was low and open too, and Sam gave him the third charge, watched him keenly, and loaded up again, and then went to the fence. The panther was lying on his side, but struggling a little; he was then within ten or fifteen feet of us, his head nearest, into which Sam lodged the fourth ball, and his race was run! We found the calf alive, but seriously injured, and returned to the house after paıtially *composing* the horse and cow. Sally had made up a fine fire—but there was no more sleep for us that night.

After daylight we went to look at the disturber of our slumbers, and found him dead enough. He measured within a few inches of nine feet from his nose to the end of his tail, and was fat enough for the butcher's stall. The flesh is often eaten by hunters, and is said to resemble mutton.

I took a good breakfast—the very double of my supper—and left my worthy host and hostess in the most kind and friendly manner.

INDIAN MOUNDS, DEER, ETC.

When I left Sam and Sally and the murdered panther, near the Yallabusha swamp, I was on a *cruise* in Upper Mississippi. Holly Springs, then just bursting into existence, was to be the *ultima thule* of my adventures north, and then the head of my horse was to be turned to the dear sunny south again.

I diverged to the right and left on my way; inquired, when I could, and examined into matters and things generally, and the lands and cotton-producing prospects particularly. That evening I crossed Yallabusha river in company with a *dare-devil* sort of a fellow, who carried a greater weight of whiskey in his saddle-bags than shirts, and who was perfectly astonished that I would not take a drink with him at least every hour from his black bottle; but I persevered in declining, with great civility and many thanks. When we reached the ferry, a very fine looking young Indian was in charge of the boat. My companion asked him, rather rudely, "You Choctaw?" I was looking earnestly at the tall and graceful "son of the forest" at the moment. He grunted deeply, *a la cochon*, and with a look, perfectly indescribable and never to be forgotten, retorted, "Choctaw, dam!" He pulled us across and received his pay without saying another word. I inquired of my *spirited* associate why the Indian thus appeared to look and express his contempt for the Choctaws.

"Why," replied he, "that fellow I knew was a Chickasaw, and hated the Choctaws, whom he looks upon as cowards; and I wanted you to see him when he expressed his feelings towards them."

The Choctaws were a quiet and friendly tribe;

and they boast of never having "shed the blood of a white man;" with how much truth I know not. Among them have been known some few very superior chiefs. Pushmatahaw, who died on his way from Washington city to the home of his fathers some years before his tribe was removed west of the Mississippi, was a man of strong *native* mind, great weight of character, and particularly eloquent; but of the Choctaws generally, the best that can be said of them is that they were harmless, inoffensive, cowardly, lazy, filthy, worthless, and ignorant in the extreme. Often, very often, have I, on falling in with a party of them, exerted myself to get some information, but the full extent and the result of all my inquiries on any subject was the eternal "*Ugh! Ugh! Ugh!*" Some of them were able to speak English so as to be understood, but never could I find one who could give me any vestige of a tradition in relation to the numerous and extraordinary mounds in their *nation*, as they always called their home and hunting-grounds. Those artificial mounds and hillocks are of various shapes and sizes, and are found in the swamps, the prairies, and forests, and no mark to designate the spot from which the earth was taken to rear up such monuments.

About twenty years since, one of those small mounds on the banks of the Yazoo river was opened, and, among other curiosities, was found the skeleton of an Indian, with an earthen covering for his entire head, fitting closely round the neck, and baked as hard as the pots and pans, which were also discovered. A most worthy and estimable gentleman present, who had ordered the digging, resolved to send the *remains, as found*, to some museum; when an Irishman, employed by him in the operation of opening the sepulchre, without any notice whatever, *smashed* the *night-cap* of the poor Indian into *smithereens*—exposing the *skull*, which was also broken by the blow.

One lovely morning, while on this *cruise*, just at sunrise, my horse started so unexpectedly that I had like to have been thrown. So soon as I recovered from the shock, I saw, not more than fifty yards from me, a number of deer—probably twenty or more. The country was an open, black-jack prairie, gently undulating. The grass was still green, and, perhaps, averaging eighteen inches high. The scene was really enchanting. The beautiful and graceful animals stood looking round for a few seconds; then, throwing back their heads, skimmed and glided over their native pastures, like fairies on a bowling-green racing by moonlight. I could see them occasionally when nearly a mile off. In ten minutes after, I saw together five more of those splendid creatures, and I cannot say how many wild turkeys I saw during that day's ride, certainly several hundred.

Towards evening I saw a low, rude pen of round logs, and what looked something like sheep lying down around it. My curiosity was excited, and I left the trace, trail, or road (as you please, reader) to examine into the matter, and when within ten feet of one corner of the pen, I assertained that the lumps, or what I thought sheep, were Indians, doubled up on the ground, and covered entirely with their blankets. Within the pen were several little hillocks or mounds of earth—two of them fresh, the others covered with grass. I spoke kindly and friendly several times and, wondering, looked upon them, but could not and did not get a reply or notice of any description, when I left them and continued my journey. I very frequently described and inquired the meaning of the exhibition, and was only enabled to get for explanation, that within the enclosure or pen were buried those Choctaws who happened to die thereabouts, and that annually certain friends or relatives of the deceased made a pilgrimage to their places of sepulture, and mourned their loss in that humble, lowly, and silent manner. There was something peculiarly melancholy and touching in the scene. No sound, no motion was heard or seen for the time, (and how long I know not.) All their hearts and souls and feelings were apparently given to the memory of departed friends and to the Great Spirit—the one mighty God of all creation. I have known no more beautiful and heavenly manifestation of affection and reverence for loved ones departed than this simple Choctaw devotion, save the unequaled and most imposing respect and splendid evidences of remembrance shown in New Orleans for deceased friends and relatives on All Saints' Day, 1st of November, annually, in the Catholic burying-grounds.

Like other forgetful and garrulous old men, I am digressing as well as diverging on my way, *n'importe, allons.* After sleeping one night in the forest, and being without food for myself *thirty-six hours*, but with grass in abundance for my horse, and meeting various little adventures during three days, I reached Holly Springs, about sunset, early in the month of October. On dismounting at a hotel, worn down by a long, hard ride, a "tall man" stepped up to me, and kindly offered to take off my saddle-bags, cloak, &c., as a servant came to take my horse. I was covered with dust, my limbs stiff and cramped from exposure to the dews and being so many hours on horseback. Indeed, I was almost inclined to think myself sick. My "tall" friend was decently dressed; and, as we walked into the bar-room, he handed my traveling *comforts* to the bar-keeper, and gave him my name, asking me immediately to take a glass of something to drink. I did not object, and as we touched glasses, he looked directly at me, and said:

"You do not recollect me?"

"I do not," I replied.

"Well, sir," said he, "I have often thought of you, and, as you may have noticed, have not forgotten your name. I met you, some months since, not far from Raymond, in Hinds county, Mississippi. I was on foot, unwell, without a cent; you gave me a dollar and some advice; do you recollect me?"

"I do recollect the meeting," said I, "but should not have recognized you; and I am happy indeed to meet you again under better circumstances."

He then imformed me that he had been robbed, and was on the track of the robber when he first met me, penniless and wearied out; but that after much suffering, he reached Natchez, where he met his brother, and there, most fortunately, caught the robber in a gambling house, and forced from him fifteen hundred dollars—within three hundred of what was stolen. That from Natchez he went to Tenessee, purchased a drove of horses, with which he was then on his way to Yazoo county, where he intended to sell his horses and purchase land to establish a cotton plantation in company with his brother, who was then with him, and who owned a few negroes.

I knew him well subsequently, saw him often, and the third year after he settled in Yazoo his crop of cotten was sold for a little over six thousand dollars.

ANECDOTES OF YAZOO AND OTHER MISSISSIPPI COUNTIES.

THE pioneers were a rude set generally, but some few intelligent and courteous gentlemen were thinly sprinkled among them. They were, however, few and far between, like angel's visits, and when I met one, it was as refreshing and delightful as the appearance of an oasis in the Great Desert of Sahara would be to an unfortunate wanderer in that waste of sand.

The manners and habits of the settlers were new and strange to me; their food was of the very coarsest description, and to add to the sufferings, I was daily reminded of the adage, that "God sends victuals, and the devil sends cooks!" for in all my previous life I had never fallen in with any cooking so villainous. Rusty salt pork, boiled or fried, "solitary and alone," like Col. Benton's ball, and musty corn-meal dodgers, rarely a vegetable of any description, no milk, butter, eggs, or the semblance of a condiment—was my fare often for weeks at a time. But little Indian corn was cultivated there in those days, and a great majority of the planters, large and small, obtained their supplies on the nearest rivers from the up-country flat boats, generally so much injured by the heat and moisture as to be unfit for a decent hog to eat. All the industry was employed in the production of cotton.

Various "towns" were located (a favorite expression in that section) in various spots; and the proprietors of all had not the shadow of a doubt (if you could believe them) that each and every one would, in a few years, contain a hundred thousand inhabitants, and that lots, seventy-five by twenty-five feet, would be worth at least twenty-five hundred dollars each; but time, a short time, dissolved, dissipated those illusions. Some of the embryo cities were removed by a single wagon to other "locations," which had their day, and were known no more forever.

Speculations in lands and negroes were of the most extraordinary character. Fortunes, in paper, were made and lost daily. A man would brag at breakfast, such as it was, that he had made fifty thousand dollars that morning, and at night would be without a dollar to brag upon, even on paper. Strange, queer, extraordinary, ludicrous, merciless, and inhuman acts and deeds were daily perpetrated. No man knew when he was safe, and nearly all went armed prepared to defend or offend.

I was among the very few who never carried a weapon, unless a decent and very reputable hickory stick could be so called; and, as astonishing as it may appear, I have often had reasons for believing that the very absence of weapons from my person was my security from insult and injury.

In the early part of 1835, one cold day, when quite a snow for that country was falling, I was compelled to take shelter for the night at a most miserable house, near the then equally miserable town of Satartia. A number of persons had passed me, or kept company with me on the road, for nearly all of us had crossed the notorious Big Black river and swamp that morning, some of whom informed me that a great race was to take place the next day, at the course near Satartia, and that some of the best horses in the State were to be competitors for large stakes.

I was advised to stop at the house mentioned, where I might get something like protection from the weather, if nothing more, but that Satartia was full to overflowing. So, as advised, I stopped with a dozen others, just after sunset, where I found about twenty more already in the house, which had two small rooms and a narrow shed—the mere shell of a building—no ceiling or plastering whatever, and only *one bed*, which was occupied by a sick female; but there were three or four miserable apologies for cots, without blankets or covering enough for one. There was one large fire-place, capacious enough for ox roasting, and a rousing fire indeed.

The miserable keeper of the establishment told us honestly those were all his accommodations; that he could feed our horses and give us the usual fare of the country, (well known to us all.) There was no option. We were like cats in a tripe shop: 'twas Hobson's choice—"That, or none;" for we were soon convinced that we could do no better in Satartia, as four unfortunates just rode up from that place to seek shelter with us.

There was but one older man than myself in the crowd, which now numbered over thirty. I saw my horse as well cared for as possible, got a "bite" of pork and corn bread for myself, which I held in my hands till finished, and fortunately obtained a seat near the fire in one corner, and did not intend to quit it during the night.

Some of the party early went into the shed, with their overcoats and horse blankets, where they endeavored to rest or sleep; but the majority, having a fair supply of whiskey, resolved to "keep it up" all night, and nearly filled the room in which the fire was burning brightly, and kept well supplied with wood during the whole night. A small table stood on the floor, at which *five* of the "blessed and unterrified democracy" of the Union took seats to play poker. I had often heard the game mentioned, but had no idea of it, except that it was a gambling game, played with cards. They had not long been at the table when a violent quarrel took place. The words used were so particularly infamous and blasphemous, that I involuntarily looked round; and at that instant I saw a man snatch or grab a handful of bank notes from the table with one hand, and a pistol, near him with the other; and then I noticed several other pistols and bowie-knives on the table. The man nearest me sprang from his seat, caught up a stick or piece of wood, more like a stave than anything else, which was leaning against the side of the chimney or fireplace just before me; and, as quick as thought, turned and raised it, evidently determined to strike some one of the gambling party. I involuntarily raised instantly, and caught him by the shoulders in front, and pressed him with all my strength against the chimney, so as to prevent him from striking, but looked him kindly in the eyes, and beseeched him to desist. He spoke not, but gave me a look I can never describe or forget. I, however, held him firmly, though several loud voices exclaimed:

"Let him go, sir. Let him strike!"

And simultaneously I heard the clicking of several pistols as they were cocked. My back was to the table. I looked round, and there were certainly six or seven pistols pointed at me and the man against the wall, and as many bowie-knives uplifted and glittering in the fire light—making, altogether, a display, a scene, that I shall never forget, and never desire to witness again.

I spoke to them as mildly as I possibly could, entreating them to put up their weapons. At that moment a voice exclaimed:

"Stranger, let him go, and stand aside, or you will be shot."

I quietly replied:

"I will not let him go while he holds the stick; and if you shoot him now, you must shoot him through me."

The fellow dropped the stick, and the only elderly man (before alluded to) present straightened himself up, and said, loud enough to be heard above all the "noise and confusion:"

"Shut up, boys—end this fuss; the stranger aint acquainted with our ways—he means good; stop it all, and drink, friends."

There was a little hesitation—silence—when one of the gamblers put up his weapons, and remarked:

"It is all right; let it go. Jim was cheated when he intended to cheat. It was a fair fight; that's the row—let's all take a drink."

The old man worked his way to me and offered his hand, which I took, as a tall young man came up, with some raw whiskey in two glasses, and said:

"Here, stranger, you and father take a drink, and we'll all be friends."

That liquor has always been my particular aversion, and I endeavored to beg off—told him I could not drink it, that it would make me sick. He looked astounded, and the old man again came to the rescue, saying:

"Don't insist on the stranger's drinking, my son."

And then, turning to me, said:

"Just touch your lips to the glass, and say let's all be friends; that will satisfy 'em."

I did so, and that scene was closed.

The gambling was not resumed, but they must do something, for it was impossible to sleep, and they chewed tobacco, smoked Kentucky cigars, and spit till the floor was a puddle.

The coming race now became the topic of conversation. There was no necessity for my talking, and I made, what is more valuable, a most patient listener. One of the party proposed that every man present should put in five dollars each to make a purse; and then write down the time that he thought the best horse would run a mile, and whoever came nearest, to receive the purse. All hands went readily into the operation. *I* was not overlooked; it would have been folly to hesitate; so I handed over my five-dollar note.

I knew, indeed, but little about horse-racing, but I knew much of horses, and had heard enough to give me an idea of the fleetness and time of running horses.

As there was nearly two inches of snow on

the ground then, the course next day, of course, would be heavy, whether the snow melted or not; so I wrote, as my time, "Two minutes." The man who handed me the paper whispered to me, and said:

"Why, stranger, they are crack horses; one of 'em is Adam Bingerman's best-blooded colt."

"Never mind," said I, "let it go."

And as he turned from me I saw him put his thumb to his nose, and signalize an associate, saying, rather louder than he intended:

"A dammed sucker."

The old man by acclamation was made the the holder of the purse.

The next day I met the persons with whom I had business, on the race-ground, and did not finish till the races were over. The sun had been shining from its rising, and rather warmly for the season. The snow was nearly gone, and the track was verry muddy; and while engaged in arranging an account on the head of a barrel in front of a tent, the old man came to wards me shouting, followed by ten or fifteen of my interesting associates of the past night; and, extending the purse, swore I was the winner, for the best horse was two minutes and two seconds in making the first mile; and no other except myself had put down over one minute and fifty seconds, and now said:

"You will give us a treat."

"Certainly," said I; "please take the purse and treat all you please to the whole amount; I am engaged, and I hope you will excuse me."

"Hilloa, stranger," he replied, "that won't do, no how; you must drink with us now; why, we can have the best French brandy here."

I did not hesitate, for I concluded the best way to get rid of the matter speedily would be to indulge the crowd. I put up my papers and followed them to a liquor stand, where the far greater part of the purse was expended in less time than would be supposed. I was called upon for a toast by the fellow who advised me to put down a less time than the two minutes; and looking at him so as to be understood, with a smile I gave:

"'*The damned sucker!*' and all his friends."

There was a general huzza—they nearly all knew what it meant. It was taken good naturedly—they all laughed heartily, and we parted in the best possible humor.

THE CHOCTAWS.

WHILE traveling in the *new purchase*, Mississippi, I often met with squads of Choctaws, and wondered at their apparent want of curiosity; sometimes I doubted their descension from Mother Eve; for nothing whatever seemed to interest them except *whiskey;* and if they ever heard of Eve's eating the apple, contrary to Divine command, they would have said her punishment was *deserved*, for not making cider of the apples and brandy of the cider, instead of greedily munching the fruit! Upon two occasions, however, I heard a few words in addition to the eternal Ugh!

At a camp-meeting, near Shongalo, Carroll

county, the first, I understood, ever held in that region, there were present, perhaps, thirty Choctaws, and a crowd of white persons, where *from*, no one (who had rode through the forests in their native wilds, as I had, without meeting with a single located democrat, sometimes, in a whole day's ride,) could imagine; but there they were, several hundred, with a goodly number of females, and no less than five of those untiring circuit riders or missionaries of the economical and enthusiastic society of Methodists, who rival the primitive Christians in the earnestness and simplicity of their devotions, and never-exhausted exertions to make converts. Their labors and privations, their poverty and perseverance, deserve success. They surpass the early Catholic missionaries who accompanied Cortez, Pizarro, and other Spanish conquerors, to the New World—at whose head stands the great, the good, the pious Las Casas. The world at large knows not the value and importance to the human race of the labor of these holy men.

There are some wolves in sheep's clothing among them, and, occasionally, bounds are wanted to the wildness or madness of their enthusiasm; but, in the main, they do much good. May heaven's blessing be upon them!

The preaching commenced quite early on the day I happened to be a spectator, as well as the poor Indians; and, about 12 o'clock, under the ranting of a fluent if not an eloquent preacher, a number of those influenced became greatly excited, particularly the females. Many of them shouted loudly, clapped their hands, tumbled down, kicked, rolled over, jumped up, tore their clothes, and were apparently frantic. I turned from the exhibition to the Choctaws, who had repeatedly grunted, "Ugh! Ugh!" very near me; when one of them, with more feathers and paint on him than any other, looked at me rather cunningly for a Choctaw, turned his head back, opened his mouth, raised his hand up to it as if drinking, and, to my astonishment, said, audibly and distinctly,

"*Hoxie! Heep whiskee—too much!*"

"Hoxie," is Choctaw for drunk. My risibles were so strongly excited by the *naive* remark, that I felt it my duty to leave the ground, being compelled to admit that a simple-minded Indian could come to no other conclusion; for such conduct could only result from or be the effect of intoxication by spirituous liquors, or derangement of intellect from some other cause, *pro tem.*

I have a great aversion to such excess, and would prefer the quiet and silent worship of the followers of George Fox to it greatly. God is not deaf, and heaven is not to be taken by storm! Be temperate in all things!

Sometime subsequently I happened, on a Sabbath, to be near where a Baptist meeting was to be held in Yazoo county, and, with several acquaintances, went to see the baptism of new converts in a well-known stream, called Wallokchebogue. On our way we overtook a small party of Choctaws, who had been hunting, and their squaws picking out cotton for some time in the neighborhood, also bound to witness the immersion, of which they understood nothing.

We were a little too late for the first scene. One of the sinners had been purified before we reached the spot, and the preacher and his followers were singing. One of the Choctaws, who spoke English enough to be understood tolerably well, inquired, with a little semblance of curiosity, the meaning of the ceremony, seeing several persons standing in the water and one thoroughly wet; when a member, (I believe he was a clergyman,) with much earnestness and patience, endeavored to explain it. The Indian at last appeared to understand that the belief was, on being dipped or covered all over in the water the believer was made perfect and holy—would sin no more, and could appear before his God, in the land of spirits, without fear of punishment: for all his crimes, and evil deeds, and thoughts, were thus washed out, and he would be the companion and brother of Jesus Christ the Saviour of Mankind!

"Ugh! ugh!" said the Indian. "Me know, me onrestan, me bobbashela quick, too."

At this moment another convert was led into the water. The clergyman, after the usual exhortation, prayers, and blessings, plunged him under, and as he did so, the now enlightend Choctaw threw off his blanket, sprang headforemost into the stream, very near the man baptized, swam under the water till he reached the opposite side, (about thirty feet,) shook himself like a water-dog, plunged in again and rose alongside of the clergyman, gave another shake, and exclaimed aloud, looking up and raising his extended hands above his head,

"*Hell exshow!* Hell exshow! Jesus Christ and me bobbashela now. Ugh! ugh!"

"*Exshow*," is Choctaw for "gone," or "lost," or "done-over," and "*bobbashela*" is "brother."

I did not laugh this time—my feelings ran another way; and I may be forgiven for thinking that following or complying with *forms or ceremonies of any description, manufactured* by man, would not, could not, make a Christian of heathenish or sinful materials! It is the heart that must be washed, the soul that must be cleansed, the spirit that must be purified, before we are prepared to be called "*bobbashela*" by the Saviour of the World. *Pure religion* depends not on the outward performance of forms and ceremonies It is felt in the hearts of all human beings; it is given to all creation; it is from God alone. He places in the breasts of His creatures a sensation of devotion, a knowledge of His power and majesty, a thankfulness for His mercies, *that is understood* according to the intelligence allotted to each; and, in their own way, however ignorant or enlightened, they honestly pour forth their gratitude, and entreat a continuance of His almighty love and protection. And whether as Jew or Gentile, Mahometan, Pagan, or Christian, he performs all the rites and ceremonies as prescribed in the *Books*, He is void of pure religion whose heart is impure!

LOCATIONS IN MISSISSIPPI, ETC.

AFTER eighteen months' cruising through this State, in search of good lands and pleasant location combined, I settled on a plantation between Yazoo and Benton. Manchester, now "Yazoo city," is on the Yazoo river, and Benton is the county-town of Yazoo. Once more will I enjoy the luxury of home, and make a paradise of this place, and have ever a warm welcome for the friends of other years who may come south in search of change, wealth, musquitoes, or alligators!

The society is not yet so good in this vicinity as around Natchez, Vicksburg, and some other places, and yet there are a sufficient number of refined and intelligent families in the neighborhood to render it agreeable.

Lawlessness is yet prevalent, as in all newly-settled countries. An instance of a man having murdered another in cold blood, and then seating himself on his victim's mangled body and enjoying a boisterous drinking song, chorused by his companions, and encored until their savage natures were appeased, would have disgraced an Indian encampment. These scenes of horror are of repeated occurrence, but time will civilize this region; and, as a good and gracious God has timed all else, it remains with man alone to make this county a second garden of Eden!

MISCELLANEOUS WRITINGS.

THE PLEASURES OF POVERTY.

"Is there for honest poverty
 Wha' hangs his head an a' that?
The coward slave, we pass him by,
 An' dare be poor, for a' that!"—Burns.

What a theme for poetry is the "Pleasures of Poverty!" Yes, the pleasures, and blessings, and benefits of poverty are unknown, unfelt by the wealthy, and the ephemeral millionaire never dreams of them; yet they exist, are valuable and numerous. Poets have sung the "Pleasures of Hope" and the "Pleasures of Imagination," but the "Pleasures of Poverty" have been unnoticed, forgotten, and unsung.

The poor man has his pleasures, his blessings, and his high hopes. He lives within himself. The fluctuations in stocks, exchanges, provisions, merchandise, lands, and estates, affect him not. Tranquillity and peace are his—the world is his! The sun shines and warms him as kindly and surely as the greatest noble of the land. The flowers bud, and bloom, and smell as sweet for him. The morning air is as fresh and sweet. His senses are as acute, yet no epicurean palate disturbs his hearty meal. He has nothing to fear and everything to hope. He is at the bottom of Fortune's wheel, and the slightest turn either way is sure to elevate him! How delightful are his prospects; how buoyant his spirits; how glorious his hopes! No treachery awaits him—no swindler locks him up! No Shylock watches his movements—no dun tracks him in his solitude or wanderings! No sheriff serves process on him—no constable taps him on the shoulder! The poor man is "o'er a' the ills o' life victorious!"

The poor man ne'er has aught to save,
  Fires may burn and tempests shatter;
No house has he, no ships, no slave!
  He sees the waste, to him, no matter,
    He's whole beyond a doubt.

Banks may fail, and stocks may fall,
  Cotton advance, decline, or stand still;
Brokers, merchants, gamblers — all
  May tramp to Hades if they will;
    He's safe, and strong, and stout.

He eats his crust, and drinks at will
  From Nature's pure unfailing spring;
No indigestion, or doctor's bill,
  Ever troubles him — an' "birdies" sing
    As sweet for him as others.

He never fears a footpad,
  Assassin, robber, midnight thief;
But whistles on his way, right glad
  That of the happy he is chief,
    And does not fear his brothers.

In poverty there are pleasures
  Unknown to men of wealth;

No change of men or measures
Affect the poor man's health—
His appetite is good.

The poor man has no hogs to feed,
In cold and snowy weather;
No cows at dawn of day to need
Both time and food together,
Through ice and frost or flood.

Poor people live on hope,
They never can be worsted;
Emp'rors, Kings, the Holy Pope!
Live in fear of being bursted,
And blown to atoms ever.

Oh, yes! there are pleasures
In poverty beyond a doubt;
For if come a change of measures,
'Tis for the better out and out;
Then let us grumble never.

But this is not all. The literature of the world is indebted to poverty for the choicest gems of poetry, history, romance, and fancy!

Poets and philosophers, artists and geniuses, from Æsop down, have reveled in the "halls" of poverty. But for the poverty of Goldsmith, the world would have never been blessed with the purest and most natural novel extant, the "Vicar of Wakefield," and the well-filled libraries of the wealthy would have never known the beauties of his "Citizen of the World," "Deserted Village," "Animated Nature," &c. But for the poverty of Smollet, "Peregrine Pickle," "Roderick Random," "Humphrey Clinker," &c., would never have delighted millions. The beauties of Otway and Savage would have never been known but for their misery and poverty.

But for the pecuniary distress (poverty) of Walter Scott, volumes of his unrivaled works would never have been written. Poverty was the main-spring of action which caused the discovery and production of numerous valuable inventions of genius, that would otherwise have slumbered ages longer in oblivion. Poverty elicits all the energies of its victims, and forces them into value, use, and importance. Fulton's poverty produced the perfection of steam power application. Franklin's poverty and dependence in himself made him one of the greatest, most useful, and most valuable of practical men that ever lived. It gave to the world his wise aphorisms, his great discoveries in philosophy, and his wonderful experience. Why, I could fill a volume with the pleasures, blessings, and rich productions of poverty. The poor are the producers of almost every good. *Vive la pauvreté!*

"What tho' on homely fare we dine,
Wear hodden grey, an' a' that;
Gie fools their silk, an' knaves their wine
A man's a man for a' that!
Thin tinsel show, an' a' that,
The honest man, tho' e'er sae poor,
Is king o' men for a' that!"

THE BRIDAL KISS.

WHEN vows are at the altar given,
  And lips can meet in mutual love;
Our hearts and thoughts are fixed on heaven,
  We have permission from above!
Then sweet, oh sweet, the bridal kiss,
  Of fearless love and blest affection;
No sigh can come to mar the bliss,
  No thought intrude to cause dejection.
The hallowed kiss of innocence,
  The kiss that riches cannot buy;
The kiss that dreads no consequence,
  The kiss that scandal may defy!
The rapturous kiss, the bridal kiss!
  So chaste, so rich, so very sweet!
'Tis heaven's gift—angelic bliss!
  When hearts as well as lips do meet!

WOMAN.

THAT women are naturally more inclined to charity (in every sense of the word) than men, there is no doubt. That females more readily sympathize with the sufferings of humanity, feel more acutely for the woes of others, and are ever more unhesitatingly prepared to relieve and attend to the afflicted than men, no one with my experience will question.

In all countries and climes and nations, woman—heavenly woman—is full of kindness, love, gentleness, and charity. Mungo Parke found it in the interior of Africa; Captain John Smith felt its influence and owed his life to it among the wild natives of the American forest.

Two hundred years ago, on the uncultivated banks of James river, an Indian girl, with native impulse alone to guide and direct her, threw herself in the way—risked her life freely, nobly, generously, kindly, to shelter a captive stranger from the death-blow of her father.

There could have been no selfishness in such an act. She could have had no idea of reward. It was an ebullition of the female heart, warmed by the God of nature into instant exertion to prevent pain and crime. Such are the deeds of woman. Who in pain or sorrow ever appealed in vain to woman's charity? What female ever closed her purse to the poor and afflicted, or refused a crust to the hungry supplicant? What cold and ragged child was ever turned away "cold and ragged" from the door—the comfortable home of a woman?

The widow's "mite" is ever ready. The woman's store is never closed. Oh, holy woman! how very much am I indebted to thee! Far, far, above all, thou must ever rank, my own dear mother, whose sheltering, tender, watchful love can never be forgotten! and my dear kind nurse, a slave, so intimately associated with my earliest recollections that they cannot be separated from her well-remembered happy face, joyous laugh, and musical voice; for until I was nine years old she was almost a part of myself—my shadow and my protector when away from my mother. Sometimes I managed to escape for a few hours, but she certainly hunted me up.

On one occasion, a most lovely morning in June, I dodged my good nurse and bounded away across the fields, in company with four boys, (one of them black,) all older than myself, to steal cherries from an orchard belonging to an old widow lady, nearly two miles from home. I was unconscious of any absolute wrong in the expedition, and was persuaded by my associates, without difficulty, to join them. We were soon in the trees without permission. I was light and active, a most excellent climber for my age, and was soon on the topmost branches, among the finest cherries, as happy as a jay-bird. How long I had been helping myself I know not, but an unusual stir induced me to look below. I saw my companions hastening rapidly down, and at the same moment heard a shout from a well known servant of the owner of the grounds, Mrs. N———. I held on quietly. The other boys escaped, and just then my nurse made her appearance. She soon understood the affair, and joined Mrs. N———'s servant in scolding me for being engaged in such an adventure. I came down and started for home. The nurse enforcing her opinion of the deed, and insisting that my mother would be very angry, and that I would certainly be punished, I reached home in tears. My mother met me at the door; inquired what was the matter, and where I had been. The tale, the truth was told; and now for the punishment. She turned to the nurse, and in a manner not to be misunderstood, said:

"Take J—— directly over to Mrs. N——'s; see that he gets upon his knees to her, and begs her pardon, and promises never to be guilty of such a thing again."

I did not perfectly comprehend the nature of such an operation; but I keenly felt I was wrong, and that something like deep degradation was to be submitted to as expiation. I knew there was no alternative; and away we went, my kind nurse and I, both in tears.

What Mrs. N—— was to do I knew not; but an awful dread was upon me, and the nearer we approached the greater were my sufferings. This time I did not go through the orchard; and as we neared the house, in front, the old lady, Mrs. N——, made her appearance on the piazza; and the nurse almost lifted me up the steps, saying in my ear:

"Now, master J——, do just as mistress told you."

I dropped on my knees at the old lady's feet,

burst into a flood of tears, and could but just make out to utter—

"Oh, Mrs. N———, I beg your pardon!"—when she caught me up in her arms, hugged and kissed me, I know not how often, carried me into her sitting-room, caressed and hushed me up; ordered some little delicacies brought for me; had a fine basket of cherries gathered for me to take to my mother, and told me, that whenever I wanted cherries to come and she would have them picked for me. There was a finale! For some time all was confusion in my mind—it was above my comprehension. Was that the way begging pardon was to end?

I feared almost to leave for home, thinking that the threatened punishment awaited me there. However, I took leave, and was repeatedly kissed at parting, and charged with numerous good wishes and kind words for my mother, who, on my reaching home, merely asked the nurse if I had behaved myself as she directed;

and on her replying affirmatively my mother called me to her side, kissed me, and said:

"My boy, you should not have acted so badly this morning; but remember, as long as you live, that it is your duty to beg pardon of any and every person you may injure or offend in any way, and you must never fail to do it."

I have never forgotten that lesson—the very first one impressed deeply on my memory by my mother, assisted by Mrs. N——— and my nurse, and the effect has never ceased its influence on my actions. This was woman's teaching. Nature has most wisely made the female heart the home of all that is good and kind, and soft and sweet. No evil is placed there by Him who "rules the whirlwind and directs the storm."

Bad women are made so by worse men, who deceive, betray, and desert them, after trifling with and playing upon their warmest feelings and richest affections; and, when women become infamous, they owe it to man's teachings.

"Auld nature swears, the lovely dears
Her noblest wark, she classes, O,
Her prentice han' she tried on man,
And then she made the lassies, O."

I WOULD NOT BE ALONE!

I ENVY not that son of God,
  Who *alone* prefers to dwell;
I'd rather be beneath the sod,
  And take my chance for heaven or hell!

I would not be a hermit, cold
  And chilly in a cave alone,
No, not for Anas' heap of gold,
  Would I *live* and be alone!

I'd rather be a *slave* and sold;
  Or be a dog to gnaw a bone;
Or be a beggar poor and old,
  Oh! sooner far than be alone!

Oh, give me something *dear* to love!
  (I have no wish for gilded throne,)
Give me *friends*, oh God above!
  And never let me be alone!

COURTESY—GENTLENESS OF MANNERS.

I WAS, in my early youth, carefully taught and soon understood the great importance and value of courtesy and gentleness of manner; and in my long, uneven passage so far through life, I have never, without previous absolute provocation, deviated the hundredth part of a hair's breadth from a kindness of manner and perfect respect to *all* persons, high or low, rich or poor, black or white, in addressing them, or replying to a respectful application or question—it matters not by whom made or put. This duty was enforced upon me when a child, and it has never been forgotten or neglected.

There is nothing more painful to a sensitive mind than the knowledge that it is neglected, unnoticed, passed over, when a consciousness exists of having made a respectful, reasonable application, or asked a necessary question in a courteous manner.

No man whose heart is in the right place, no Christian, when in possession of a little ephemeral power, clothed with a *little* brief authority, tricked out with an evanescent robe of honor, would look upon his fellow-worm, (uncovered with tinsel show,) as beneath him, and not deserving his notice. In this highly favored Union, such are the vicissitudes of life, that the high and low often and rapidly change places! And yet, poor human nature, such fantastic tricks are cut by *some* of our fleeting nobility (*pro temp.*) as often cause the meek and humble to shed the scalding tear of bitter pain! The honorable, *for the day*, forgets his God, his duties, and his grave! You knock at his door in vain! You appeal to him without notice! You ask of him, through his satellites, and receive no answer! The lords of the land only, as his *equals*, receive his prompt attention! He dreams not who *may* be his equals on the next swing of the pendulum—the next flow of the waters! God only is great! Man, however high in office to-day, is but as the tiny insect which appears, crawls, is missed, and gone forever! And yet, in his short breathing time on earth, how much of agony, unnecessarily, does man cause man for want of a small share of attention, kindness, courtesy, and gentleness of manner.

A soft and kind word in reply, at the proper moment, uttered with gentleness of manner, might heal the wounds of a broken-hearted supplicant. Courtesy costs but little, and its absence often causes much sorrow, pain, and distress. "Soft words turneth away wrath;" and when a favor is *refused*, if done in a kind and gentle manner, no sting is left behind to pain and rankle—no open wound is tortured and inflamed.

The rudest heart, the roughest exterior, is won by courtesy and kindness of manner. A gentle expression of reply or recognition is never lost on any human being; and all domesticated animals not only understand but appreciate kind and gentle words.

When a gentleman is respectfully addressed orally or by letter by a man, however humble his station in life may be, the applicant has a natural and inalienable right to a reply. It is a duty necessarily imposed on society, and should never be omitted or neglected where courtesy and mutual civility can only prevent numerous outrages.

A man of sense and reason will ever address *slaves or servants*, civilly, decently, courteously, and reply to them in the same manner, and will never permit them to remain in attendance *unnoticed.* No taunt of superiority, no word of contumely from a gentleman, should ever reach, to wound the ear or pain the heart of an inferior, whose duties are faithfully performed. Orders and requests by those in power should ever be given and made in courteous and respectful terms. "*Suaviter in modo fortiter in re.*"

On my way to Charleston, S. C., in 1819, the stage stopped for the *two* passengers to dine at a miserable village near a branch of the Pedee. Quite a crowd of persons, apparently much excited, were around a small house two squares off; and I, with a little of Mother Eve's curiosity, walked towards the spot, and inquired civilly at first, without being heard or noticed; but on getting pretty near the house, I asked in a most kind and gentle manner what was the cause of such an assemblage. Before I received a reply, a man in the house opened a shutter about half way, presenting such a face as I never beheld before. There was fear, horror, crime, vengeance, hatred, almost everything vile, clearly exhibited in it. My heart melted at the picture, and I approached the window with pity, compassion, and sorrow so evident in my manner, that the miserable man understood it—the whole crowd shouting to me to keep away, that he would shoot me; that he had murdered his wife, was armed, had defied the law's power, and that the sheriff and his deputy were then expected with an armed posse to storm the house and take him by force. I walked calmly to the window, looking directly in the poor wretch's eyes, as charitably and kindly as I possibly could. He had fought his way through the crowd but an hour before, had been much beaten and abused, and by great exertions got into the house and fastened himself in. As I placed my hand on the window-sill, he softly said:

"Stranger, they want to kill me; they want to hang me without knowing the truth."

I replied instantly, and without authority, of course:

"Oh, no! certainly not—they are men; they

will, I know they will, give you a legal and fair trial. They only wish you to submit to the law. Resist no more. When the sheriff comes, receive him kindly. Give me your weapons. I know nothing of what you are charged with, but be advised by me, and I know you will be treated kindly."

The poor fellow burst into tears—caught my hand and kissed it, and exclaimed:

"Oh, my God! you have spoken the first kind words to me that I have heard for months, and I will do as you wish."

He immediately opened the door and I stepped in. No one attempted to follow me, and only one man in all that assembly uttered another uncivil or harsh word, for which he was rebuked instantly by several near him. The sheriff, *alone*, at that moment turned the corner, and saw me standing in the door with a pair of pistols and a large butcher or carving knife, just handed me by the murderer, who was near me, with the big salt tears rolling down his cheeks, and I not much better off. The sheriff addressed him mildly and feelingly; and without another cruel, insulting, or harsh word, he was then taken quietly to prison. I was dressed in black, (not so common in those days,) and the first expression I heard, after leaving the house, was:

"If it had not been for that preacher, Tom K—— would never have left that house alive."

WOMAN'S GLANCE.

WHEN looking on the fairy throng,
  We early meet the magic glance
From woman's eyes in syren song,
  Or whirling in the mazy dance.
    How deep it strikes, how quick and strong,
      How thrilling to the heart it goes!
    Oh! he who lives on love and song
      And woman's thoughts most surely knows.
  'Tis brilliant as the lightning's flash,
    And oh! as fatal sometimes too;
  It kills us at a single dash,
    Or tells us—live, and love, and woo!

REMINISCENCES OF MY BOYHOOD.

I KNOW not how old I was, but certainly, when my father first lectured or counseled me on the indulgence of my passion or temper, I was very young, for he was not fully understood or comprehended until after frequent explanatory discourses; and I distinctly remember how difficult it was for me to accord with him, notwithstanding, and carry out or comply with his advice or follow his instructions.

I had a *tit-for-tat* disposition, but was not at all quarrelsome, peevish, fretful, or captious, and never was harsh or combative without a sufficient provocation, in my opinion; but I was sometimes punished and more frequently chided for my childish and boyish disputes and contests. My father impressed it upon me in a *striking* manner that I must not and that it was cowardly and mean to strike a boy who was younger and smaller than myself, however such boy might provoke, injure, or insult me. But when I earnestly yet *naively* asked him if a larger or older boy should strike or injure me what I was to do, he, perhaps without due reflection, instantly replied:

"Knock him down, if you can, with whatever you can put your hands on!"

This instruction I understood, and did not forget, for it was to my unsophisticated mind perfectly natural, and savored of sweet revenge.

I was, perhaps, eleven years old, at the country school near my childhood's dear home—my teacher a kind, pleasant, and intelligent Scotchman, who is ever remembered with pleasure. I was quite a favorite with the master and nearly the whole school. I was always dressed neatly, and had a passion absolutely for keeping myself clean.

Nothing whatever annoyed me more than getting my clothes soiled in any way, and although I joined heartily in all the amusements and plays of the other boys, I ever avoided mud and dirt.

One day, after a rain, we were engaged in some game or other, running about the ground and public road in front of the school-house, when a boy several years my senior, and much stouter and stronger, without any cause whatever, threw mud on me—not much, but quite enough to soil my clothes and to mortify me. I remonstrated, and, under the circumstances, in a very mild manner; and to my astonishment, instead of expressing sorrow or regret, he caught me up in his arms in an angry manner, and swore he would throw me in a deep ditch near by. I struggled with all my might to get away from him. Nearly every boy present begged and entreated him to let me go. He approached the muddy drain; my face was close to his, and I saw evil intent in his eyes. I clung to him as if in a death-struggle, and looking firmly at him said, entreatingly—

"Do not put me in."

"I will," said he, and he lowered his head as he spoke, when I instantly caught his chin in my mouth, and as quick as thought my teeth were in contact with his jaw-bone, above and below. I shut my eyes, and no bull-dog ever gripped his victim with more savage tenacity or ferocity. He yelled aloud, screamed, and begged. I felt his blood running down my neck—it mattered not. The boys shouted and huzzaed. The poor devil fell on the ground, rolled over and let me go, but I only held the tighter to him and bit him the harder. I felt and knew "I had him," and that "sweet revenge" was mine.

The master came out, and the boys gave him a true version of the affair. He walked up to us, both on the ground. I looked him calmly in the eyes, still without loosening my hold or teeth. He stooped down, patted me gently on the head, and said, in his richest Scotch dialect:

"Loot him gang, Jamie, lad, he has gotten joost what he desarved, frae a' I can learn; an' I'se warrant he'll na' attempt till thraw ye i' the mud again."

I let go and rose up. My antagonist was humbled, absolutely conquered, and was laughed at by the whole school.

I rather feared my father, and knew not how he might feel or act in consequence of my taking such signal vengeance on a playmate, though he was so much older and larger than myself, and had so grossly insulted and injured and intended further to injure me. But the good teacher saw my father before evening, purposely, and gave him such a ludicrous account of the affair, (I learned subsequently,) that he laughed very heartily, and never said a word to me on the subject.

The poor fellow carried the marks, the fair and full impression of my teeth on his chin, (above and below,) to his grave. And yet I cannot say that I ever regretted punishing him as I did. I never had any respect for him, and he always, so long as he lived, appeared ashamed or mortified to meet me; and after I was grown up, he never thought of attempting "till thraw me i' the mud again, I'se warrant ye!"

Some twelve months or more after the above incident, I was at the academy in our county town, where there were about one hundred scholars. I was very active, a good runner, and expert at most of the games of amusêment indulged in by the boys, and was always among the first chosen when making parties for any play.

At bandy or shindy, one day, I was on the side opposed to a large boy, or almost young man—for he was five or six years older than me—and in a hard race for a ball, I was just in the act of striking it, when, to prevent me, he struck my foot rather severely. I lost the ball, but I gave him the blow with all my strength in his face. He reeled or staggered off ten or twelve feet, but recovered in a few seconds, and came angrily towards me, with his bandy raised. I stood as still and was as white and cold as a statue of Parian marble. I expected to be knocked down and severely beaten, but I resolved to strike once more if I died for it. He was bleeding freely from his mouth and nose, and when almost near enough to reach me, he suddenly stopped, threw his bandy down, and said, impressively:

"No, I will not strike you, I was wrong when I struck your foot; I ought not to have done it, and I deserved the blow you gave me."

I burst into tears, and could but just utter:

"I am verry sorry I struck you so hard."

He caught me by both hands, and said:

"You are a good boy, I—I was to blame; let us be friends."

I went to the pump with him. He washed

and bathed his face till the blood ceased to flow, and I then accompanied him to his boarding-house.

That man has ever been my friend since, and there is but one other in this wide world to whom I am more indebted for kindness and obligations when they were needed. I have loved him from that time as a brother. He is yet living. May heaven spare him many years of usefulness, generosity, and charity, free from pains and sorrows, and may all his declining days be peaceful and happy.

These two adventures of boyhood present a striking contrast, and may be profitably compared and reflected on by the youthful of the present day.

Boys should never injure or insult their playmates—there is no necessity for it whatever They should exert themselves and struggle to forgive little misunderstandings and apparent wrongs and *gaucheries*, and passion should never be permitted to obtain the mastery in consequence of trifling difficulties.

There are but few children whose parents do not often give them good advice, and nearly all the evils and sorrows that attend the young are caused by disobedience or forgetfulness of parental counsel.

YOUTH.

Oh! this world is light and green
  When our hopes and joys are young,
On the brightest side all things are seen,
  And far away all cares are flung.

The sea is green—the leaves are green—
  All is green and fresh and fair;
It is always May, oh! lovely scene—
  Green fields—green things are everywhere.

No spot is dark, in view no cloud,
  No thought to interrupt the truth;
And lightly bounds the heart so proud
  In young and happy, careless youth.

But age will come—the sight will fade,
  The green things dark appear;

When all things lovely God has made,
  Will dark and gloomy look, I fear.

Then turn your thoughts to higher things
  In youth's gay, careless, happy hours;
When there's a change, then time will bring
  A *crown* of bright celestial flowers!

CHILDREN AND GHOST STORIES.

My good nurse had at least one fault—a fondness for telling raw-head and bloody-bones stories. I am sure she never had an idea of the least wrong in such an amusement, but the effect on me was a cruelty; for often have I gone to bed trembling with terror, and covered my head for fear of seeing something horrible.

My father knew not that any fears of that description withered my heart; and one night, on telling me to perform some little errand for him, he noticed my hesitation or reluctance; and as I had always been taught and did obey him implicitly and immediately, he called me to him, and earnestly asked me if I was afraid to go alone in the dark, and if I thought he would send me if there was any danger whatever? I endeavored to get round the question, but tears filled my eyes and ran down my cheeks, and I made a full confession of my fears and the cause of them. My nurse was called, lectured very severely, and threatened with being turned out of the house if she ever again told tales or stories to frighten me. She obeyed, for nothing is more degrading to, or considered a greater punishment by, a good servant accustomed to the house, than to be turned out and put in the field under an overseer.

But the effect of her nightly stories were deeply engraven on my heart, and for years when left alone in bed without a light I suffered.

My father reasoned with me, encouraged me, told me many anecdotes about the ludicrous discovery and exposition of what were thought to be ghosts. He convinced me that of all the ghosts ever said to have been seen or heard of, none had ever injured a human being; and then he said—

"Should you ever see or hear anything in the night which you cannot understand without, go directly up to it, take hold of it, and my word for it you will not find a ghost."

He then said to me "When Old Conestoga (a favorite horse) was about three years old, and as I thought tolerably well broken, I rode him one cold day down to the Sound, to shoot wild geese and ducks; and having been fortunate, I was out till after night; but the moon was nearly full, and shining beautifully bright. On my return home I crossed an old field, the bridle-path through which passed very near a grave-yard, which had been neglected for many years. Conestoga suddenly started back, snorted, raised his head, and could not be induced to move forward. I coaxed, soothed, patted him, all to no purpose. I then spurred him sharply and quickly, but he reared up and still refused to go ahead, apparently much alarmed. I ceased operations for a moment, looked searchingly around, and discovered something which I thought was a sheep between two graves, and heard at the same instant a low moan or groan. I knew that was what had frightened the horse. I dismounted and endeavored to lead him to the spot, but he was not to be led or driven. I took him a small distance in another direction, fastened him to a sapling, and went up to the cause of my difficulty, when I found it was a man, and on taking hold of him to ascertain his condition, I recognized a poor drunken Irishman, well known in the neighborhood for his dissipated habits. He had straggled from the main road, fallen where I found him, was asleep, and in all probability would have never lived to get drunk again but for Conestoga's fear of ghosts! He was rather sober when I raised him up, but I had much difficulty in getting him home with me and quieting the alarm of Conestoga.

"Now, my boy," said my father, "there's a

better ghost story than you ever heard before. Don't forget it. If I had believed in ghosts as firmly as my horse, we should have both run away, left poor Paddy to freeze to death, and believed all our lives we had seen a ghost."

That story relieved me greatly, and although I often had fears of ghosts and hobgoblins subsequently, my father did not suspect me, and ultimately my pride fairly conquered my fears; and before I was much older, however my fears operated, I never hesitated at all hazards to examine into every cause of alarm that presented itself. Several queer and some ludicrous exposures were the result; and more than one rather strange adventure I could relate perhaps to advantage.

It is, perhaps, near forty years since, that, on a clear cold, star-light night in the fall, I had to gallant an elderly maiden lady home, who had been attending a sick female friend. Our way was by the old Colonial Church of the southern town in which I then resided. We passed the yard, (which occupied a whole square, in the center of which stood the sacred pile.) I saw her safely housed, and immediately left. On returning along the church-yard fence, which was made of thick, heavy, pitch-pine plank, darkly painted, and placed horizontally about two inches apart—one of these interstices being even with my eyes—I saw a tall figure, as of some person with a sheet thrown over the head and hanging down to the feet, standing on a well-known tombstone, where reposed the remains of a man who was the friend of my boyhood, and whom I loved almost as my father. The tomb was not more than fifteen feet from the fence; and when I got directly opposite, I looked through the fence at the object composedly. It was then about 2 o'clock A. M. There was the figure, plain, distinct, and motionless.

I rubbed my eyes, looked again; there it was. I was convinced it was no delusion. I determined to know what it was and what it meant, if possible; and, mounting the fence quickly, asked, audibly and distinctly,

"Who is that, and what do you mean by being in such a place at such a time?"

No reply. I instantly jumped off the fence towards the tomb, exclaiming: "I'll know who or what you are," as I jumped. The figure leaped from the tomb on the opposite side, threw the sheet or whatever it was, from its head, and ran off over the uneven ground with a speed that bid fair to distance me, hallooing out—

"If you hadn't known I was alive you never would have come into this church-yard."

After falling three times in the sunken graves and being fairly beaten, I gave up the chase; I knew the voice. It was that of a somewhat strange, stout negro woman belonging to a widow lady in the town. As she ran I threatened her severely, but I never found out why she was there, and to this day the extraordinary act is above my comprehension; but the ghost was "blown up;" the very pith and marrow of the story destroyed by my exertion and exposure.

It is almost impossible to prevent children from hearing tales or stories that frighten them, and the effects remain in some forever. Parents should guard against such things with constant care; the evil is great indeed, for I have often met persons, men and women of mature age, who had the courage to acknowledge their fear of ghosts, goblins, etc.; and among them was Captain Otway Burns, of the celebrated Snap-Dragon Privateer, who was so very gallant and successful in the war of 1812. He feared nothing living; no odds deterred or daunted him; and yet, in consequence of his childhood impressions, he feared to the day of his death to be left alone at night in a room without a light.

There is unmitigated cruelty in thus enslaving a child. I was certainly sixteen or seventeen years old before my sufferings and fears ceased, although my pride for some years previous enabled me to conceal them.

From the time my father first lectured and reasoned with me on the subject, I struggled hard for freedom from the nightly terrors that distressed me. I was convinced beyond a doubt that there was no shadow of cause for my fears, yet so strongly and deeply were they impressed on my mind that the difficulty was not entirely overcome for many years; and often, when nothing could prevent me from going in the dark on any purpose whatever, my sensation would, to say the least, be very unpleasant, and I would deeply regret the origin.

Parents should question their children, and early remove the slightest impression of such fears; and nurses and associates should be cautioned against and punished if detected for telling ghost, witch, and raw-head and bloody-bones stories.

TIME ALONE CAN CURE.

'Tis said that time can conquer *pain,*
  And sorrows, woes, and troubles;
That time can *peace* restore again,
  And tranquilize life's bubbles,
          That boil and fret us oft

'Tis said that *time* cures all the ills
  That life and flesh are heir to;
That God for *good* his *pleasure* wills-
  And all receive a share, too,
          Before we're called aloft.

'Tis surely true—then do not grieve
  Whatever ills attend you;
You'll be prepared before you leave—
  Yes, Heaven will befriend you
          Before you're called aloft.

REVENGE AND MALICE.

WHEN stricken on one cheek, it is hard indeed to believe it our duty to turn the other calmly and court a duplicate. But few have courage enough to practice this Christian virtue; for sinful human nature revolts at what is felt to be degrading and cowardly submission to insults and injuries as understood in nearly all societies.

Injuries may be forgiven and forgotten, but insults never can. Christ taught the forgiveness of both. They are often forgiven but seldom forgotten by the sensitive sufferer. We should most sincerely pray that a desire for revenge or a feeling of malice should never remain for a moment in our hearts. No good can come of it. Nothing but evil, sorrow, and regret, can ever follow an indulgence in such passions. A cold-blooded nursing of enmities will generally end in violent crime of such magnitude that "purgatory may not expiate."

Injuries from our fellows must be forgiven, if we hope or expect forgiveness from the God of Heaven, whom we are ever offending, whose commandments we are ever breaking, whose teachings we are ever disregarding, and whose punishment we ever deserve. No mortal can be perfect. There is none good but God—there is nothing true but heaven.

When about ten years of age, I was attending a school in the country near my childhood's home, in charge of a man named N———, who was a low-bred and rather vulgar fellow, with much more presumption than education or intellect, and who often neglected his duties to enlighten his pupils, as he thought, by relating to them the heroic deeds and great wealth of his ancestors. One day he was giving an account most minutely of a terrible fight with the Indians, in which he (at that time in his sixteenth year) and his father were engaged, The prodigies of valor performed by them, the number of "red-skins" killed and wounded by them, and the gaping tomahawk wounds received in return, had deeply interested all his juvenile auditors, when a little girl, always queer in manner, left her seat and approached the gallant warrior. On getting very near him, she attracted his attention, and with the utmost *naivete* asked—

"Did'nt you get killed and scalped, Mr. N———?"

From my early boyhood I never could resist a hearty laugh, when anything ludicrous, amusing, or witty was seen or heard; and I, with others, laughed outright. Silence was sternly commanded, but another cachinatory explosion involuntarily burst from me. I had ever been attentive to my lessons; had never been reprimanded punished, or scolded by the master; and no boy in the school had been more diligent or better prepared for recitations or examination than I. Two days subsequently, on Friday, after he opened as usual his black book, as he called his record of offences, and after calling up some half dozen offenders and punishing them, to my astonishment and mortification he called *me!* I was perfectly unconscious of having been guilty of the slightest deviation from his rules, and I walked up calmly, looking him full in the face.

"Take off your jacket, sir," said he, in the most brutal manner.

"What am I to be punished for?" I inquired, quivering with sensations never felt before.

"For laughing out in school, sir," he replied.

Nature triumphed, and I buttoned up my jacket, looking "rattlesnakes" at him, without blinking or moving a muscle of my face; for I dared to think I did not deserve a whipping for that offence, if offence it could be called. The brute sprang from his seat, caught up five large beech switches, and scourged me cruelly, repeatedly and loudly exclaiming—

"Won't you beg, sir?"

A relative in school, much older than I was, almost halloed out—

"Why don't you beg, you little fool?"

I would have suffered death first; and then, for the first time during the punishment, I turned my eyes from the master to my cousin, looking vengeance at him. No word, no cry of pain escaped my lips, and no tears filled my eyes.

When the savage had sated his vengeance, or was fatigued with his exertions, he shoved me nearly across the room, where I fell. A sweet girl, several years my senior, helped me up, and without obstruction, walked out into the yard with me; burst into tears, folded me in her arms and kissed me! Up to that moment no sound had escaped my mouth—no feeling had room in my heart but vengeance; and in my soul I swore, if ever God gave me strength and opportunity, I would lacerate that man's back more severely than he had mine! Tears then came to my relief; the school was dismissed, and my female friend accompanied me to my father's gate and left me. She yet lives, and I have never ceased to love her with the pure and holy love of a brother.

My kind and good old nurse (who still attended to my clothes, and nightly assisted to undress me) saw how I was bruised and beaten, and immediately informed my mother, and they both had a hearty cry while washing and anointing me. My father was not about, and on his return some weeks after, I prevailed on my mother not to inform him of the outrage. Revenge was mine. My heart gloated in it, and I could not bear the idea that my father should participate in it; and I rather doubted or feared he would say my obstinacy in not begging deserved the punishment inflicted, for he was a strict disciplinarian. Time passed;

N——— left the county, and all others save me, perhaps, had forgotten my undeserved punishment.

Nine years elapsed. Nearly half of them I spent in the city of New York, and returned to my native home, with vengeance still alive, and almost welling over in my heart. I inquired for N———, and ascertained he was living in an adjoining county, about thirty-six miles off. Although my heart during the time had melted with charity and kindness a thousand times, there was that one dark spot yet in it; and whenever the memory of N——— passed over my mind, the desire for revenge was apparently strong as ever. I knew the neighborhood well in which he lived. I was strong and active, and in excellent health. I purchased a superior, new, keen cowhide, mounted my horse early one morning, and in the evening was at his next door neighbor's, an old acquaintance and friend of my boyhood. I asked all the necessary questions, and among other information, I learned that N——— had long been in bad health and was very poor.

Immediately after breakfast the next morning, I walked over with revenge and malice yet in my soul and the cowhide in my hand. On nearing the house, I saw a person sitting in the front porch; and notwithstanding his squalid and miserable appearance instantly knew it was N———, the intended victim of my long pent-up vengeance. As I approached him he looked very steadily at me, and attempted to rise, but fell feebly back in the chair, saying—

"Why, isn't that J—— C——? Well, how glad I am to see you. Why, what a man you are grown to be; do take a seat. I have not heard from you since you went to New York. Do take a seat; you see I am not long for this world," extending his shriveled hand to me.

If I had murdered him, and his ghost at midnight had stood at my bedside and aroused me from balmy sleep, my feelings, my sensations could not have been more horrible! The revulsion or reaction was so violent, that I actually fell on the floor insensible; and for fifteen minutes or more I knew nothing. Mrs. N——, his wife, had raised my head, placed a pillow under it, had thrown vinegar in my face, and was rubbing my hands, when I became conscious, and N—— was crying like a child.

It was nearly two hours before I was able to walk; when my old friend at whose house I had stopped, came to look me up, and carried me home in his carriage, where I remained two days—N—— sending over repeatedly to know how I was.

I left them, and I never had the courage to tell any one there the object of my visit, nor was it ever suspected. Had I found N—— in good health, I should have committed an outrage which might have been a source of sorrow and misery forever; and I thanked God, from the core of my heart, that my hunt for revenge terminated as it did.

That was another lesson which I have never forgotten. When I have been provoked, injured, or insulted, that transaction would ever recur to my mind, and no after revenge has ever since soiled a spot in my heart; no malice can live in my breast. Let all, if any, who may read this true memoir, remember that revenge belongs not to man, and that malice is an attribute of the evil one. For nine years did the most vile of human passions dwell in my bosom; but the result of my visit for revenge cured me forever! For years, whenever the adventure was called to my mind, tears involuntarily filled my eyes, and I would thank God I had escaped so well.

HOPE.

THO' clouds o'ercast and tempests mar
  Too oft our fondest dreams;
Tho' grief and pain and savage war
  Destroy our brightest schemes—
The saddest gloom will pass, they say;
  Calms closely after storms are found;
Sunbeams chase the clouds away,
  And quiet peace comes gently round.

HUSBAND AND WIFE.

How holy, how sacred should the ties that bind husband and wife together in this world be guarded, preserved, and remembered! The confiding, trusting, loving wife leaves parents, brothers, sisters; early friends and associates; the home of her childhood, the play-grounds of her youth; her heart devoted to her husband, but welling over with grief at leaving all her early loves. She gives her all to the husband of her choice, the future partner of her joys and sorrows. She voluntarily promises to love, honor, and obey him, in sickness and in health in poverty and affliction; and he promises to nourish and protect and provide for her, and to love her only till death, aye, death! Nothing else severs the ties.

The marriage contract is more sacred, more important than any other social obligation known to the civilized world. It deserves and should command and receive more respect; and that bond should never be broken, repudiated, nullified, or forgotten.

In the marriage ceremony, however varied in the customs of the numerous nations, societies, and tribes of the earth, civilized and natural, (or barbarous,) there is in all the varieties a solemnity (more or less) always impressive, however wise, or simple, or imposing; there is ever an awe or seriousness in the performance, carrying conviction to the heart of every spectator that the institution is of heavenly origin, and that it should not be entered into carelessly, without reflection, and without the earnest intention of both parties to faithfully perform their voluntary pledges and obligations; that the sacred bonds should not be given ignorantly; and that all the duties should be understood and duly weighed ere the irrevocable act of consummation.

The marriage alliance should never be entered into lightly and thoughtlessly, giddily or playfully, as if it were a frolic. It is for life, and much good or more evil is the certain consequence. Very young persons are incapable of selecting partners or companions for life; and although generally early marriages are advisable and best, yet I would oppose parental authority to the marriage of young masters and misses. A man had better be over twenty-five years of age, and a female over nineteen than under. And in all cases males and females, young or old, should avoid a fool with a pretty face when selecting a wife or husband. Cleanliness of person, activity of mind and limbs, with a fair share of common sense on both sides, are the most certain guaranties of happiness in a married life. Fools scold and fret and frown and fume or pout for trifles.

No man of sense would quarrel with his wife

whether the turkey should be boiled or roasted for dinner; no woman of sense would quarrel with her husband because he preferred rolls to muffins for breakfast.

"Marriage has many pains," doubtless, and their numbers are greatly increased by the parties for want of common sense, reflection, kindness of disposition, charity and forgiveness. Ignorance of duties and selfishness, bad temper, thoughtlessly indulged in, drive away reason, and frequent repetitions make marriage a curse.

Husbands and wives should never contradict, positively, rudely, or passionately, each other. There is no necessity for it, and good can never come out of it. No husband should ever neglect any little pleasant attentions to his wife. They are due and are expected. No wife should forget to receive her husband pleasantly when he returns from business, or neglect to have his little customary wants ready for him on his arrival after any absence.

Mutual civilities and kindnesses are invaluable parts of the rights belonging to married persons, and the party neglecting to tender them on all occasions commits the first breach in the marriage contract. Petty, contemptible, and vulgar jealousies should never find a resting-place in the hearts of married persons who respect and guard themselves; and all and every cause for such ridiculous suspicions should be most scrupulously guarded against.

In associations with our fellows we may and should tender to all every courtesy, civility, and attention the usages of society require, pleasantly and acceptably, without subjecting ourselves, or deserving the charge or suspicion of what causes jealousy.

A man of sense is ever pleased to see gentlemen attentive to his wife. It is proof of her worth, and that she is properly esteemed. A man of sense will never neglect his wife in society; and a wife should ever be pleased to see her husband attentive to ladies who are neglected and require attentions.

RELIGION AND FRIENDSHIP.

RELIGION and friendship may soften
  The soul, when troubled and sore;
But when visited dearly so often,
  The heart will sigh for yet more.

A blank, a waste is around it,
  A loneliness — a desolate chill;
Religion and friendship surmount it,
  But the *heart* is a dreariness still.

It sighs for what it has cherished;
  It throbs' for loved ones above;
It weeps for those that have perished,
  And sighs for something to love.

Sweet glow of bright cheering friendship,
  Oh, would that ye could bid depart

The shadow that falls o'er my spirit,
  And the chill that now binds my heart.

But even when blest and sincerest
  With kindness and love running o'er,
The soul may feel it the dearest,
  But the heart will sigh for yet more.

A MOTHER'S LOVE.

There dwells not in the human breast a passion so holy, so pure, so sincere, so lasting, so strong, so devoted, so fearless of consequences under all circumstances or difficulties and dangers, as a mother's love for her child. For her child a mother will dare do anything that mortal power can. A sick child is sure of its mother's sleepless vigils, and ceaseless care and attention. In starvation, the last morsel of food is placed in the child's mouth, and she dies with the last prayer breathing for its happiness. She will protect it from cold with her feeble, attenuated form, and the last rag of want and misery left. She will snatch from danger, unhesitatingly, her child, regardless of life herself. At the risk of all, she meets and braves a tiger or a wasp with equal indifference, should it be exposed to either. When disease, sorrow, and poverty oppress her, she labors for it till death stiffens her nerves. Ingratitude, crime, dissipation, neglect, abuse from a child, weighs not a feather upon the mother's heart—she loves, and loves forever. Upon the gallows, ironed, in a dungeon, under sentence of death for the most ignominious act in the catalogue of infamy, detested, shunned, and hated by all else, the mother clings to, endeavors to console and encourage, and loves her child. Husband, parents, friends of early youth are forgotten, but a mother never forgets her child. There is nothing selfish in a mother's love. A child may love its parents, but age weakens it—a sister may love a brother, but a husband obliterates that love, and the brother is forgotten. *Nothing* destroys a mother's love—she loves her child forever. However delicate, sensitive, or cowardly a mother may be apparently, in matters where her babe is not interested, she ever displays a Spartan heroism, a gallant bearing and chivalrous demeanor, a presence of mind worthy the greatest Roman of them all, when danger threatens. Prompt, decisive, and judicious action is the first impulse when she sees or hears her child in peril.

An infant had crawled near a precipice; its mother saw it with agony and horror, yet she screamed not—she did not faint; no, she approached it calmly, called it by its pet name, softly and sweetly, baring at the same instant to view her breast; when the child turned and crowing with delight, clapped its tiny hands, and scrambling gleefully to its fount of nourishment, was soon in its mother's arms.

Any good soldier could dare the cannon and cross the bridge of Lodi, as did Bonaparte; any good soldier could mount and storm the walls of a well-defended fortress—the leader of a forlorn hope; but no man, no father, could have, under such circumstances, commanded his presence of mind—he would have rushed at the risk of his own life to the rescue, and as he leaped, instead of catching, would have frightened his child into an involuntary forward motion, and to instant destruction.

A mother, only, is ever prepared, composed, and wise enough to save and protect her child when dangers threaten; a mother, only, is blessed with more than mortal energies at such moments; and after all is over and safe, she swoons and resuscitates WOMAN, apparently feeble and dependent on the self-styled lords of creation! Oh, holy, heavenly mother! how much do I owe thee! If in me there is aught of good, it is from my mother's teachings, my mother's examples; if ever I sinned or erred, it was because my mother's advice was unattended to, neglected, forgotten. Oh, sainted mother! how very dear to me is thy memory!

I have long and painfully known the world.

I have lost parents, brothers, sisters, wife, sons, and daughters; grief and sorrows have bowed me down and silvered my hair; time has thrown his mantle over me and softened the throbs of agony, calmed and soothed my aching heart, but the memory of my mother's love, and care, and advice, and looks, is yet fresh and green.

"MAN WANTS BUT LITTLE HERE BELOW."

"Man wants but little here below,"
  The poet sweetly sings,
And all that he should want to know
  Comes down on angels' wings.

From Heaven comes all knowledge, good
  To mortals who desire;
And he who loves his Maker, should
  For wisdom there inquire.

In ignorance we are born, no doubt,
  Our eyes are blindly closed;
The earth is ours, we creep about
  And *feel*—when we're disposed.

But farther, when the stars and sun
  In glories shine forever,
How little do we know of ONE
  Who made them—living ever!

CHARITY.

True charity should fall, like the blessed dew of heaven on the parched verdure of the earth, quietly and refreshingly on its recipients, without shouts and exulting publications.

Ostentatious charity has its reward on earth, and deserves none in the world above. God has made it the imperative duty of those whom he blesses with riches to bestow charity; but in giving to the poor and needy, it is better that the "right hand should know not what the left hand doeth." The man of wealth, who accompanies his gifts by boasting proclamations, blazoned abroad in the daily journals, stands on the books of Heaven with an account fairly balanced—nothing to his credit on the score of charity is there.

"Charity covers a multitude of sins"—aye, the heaven-born charity, the heartfelt charity, the charity that comes from the soul freely and noiselessly, to give life and health and peace to the broken-hearted, poor, helpless sufferer; to stay the bitter pang and scalding tear of sorrow and grief; to calm the agony of an afflicted mother, and make her fatherless and starving children leap and clap their attenuated hands with joy to them unknown before! The charity that is acknowledged in Heaven, and there credited the donor, is pure and free from selfishness; it relieves the afflicted, aids the sufferer, and comforts the needy, without a boastful display to the world of such acts. The exhibition destroys the saint-like value of true charity, and the giver has his only reward in worldly notoriety.

True charity searches for its objects. No bluster, no trumpeting, no publication precedes the heavenly wanderer, as he silently perambulates the lanes and alleys and by-ways of wretchedness, poverty, want, disease, and sorrow. He finds and relieves the sufferer, returns quietly with a double blessing attending him to his bed of peaceful slumber; all, save God and his own pure heart, ignorant of the falling of the dew, and the receiver alone murmuring prayers of thankfulness to the unknown comforter.

The millionaire who gives his thousands to aid in building hospitals and houses of refuge for the poor and afflicted, the crippled and insane, the widow and orphan, does indeed much good in the sight of God, and will have his reward here and hereafter. The poor man, with limited means, the laborer who has a family to support, and yet spares from his pittance a "mite" for the sick and afflicted cheerfully, while his heart overflows for the sorrow before him, and deep regret that he has not more to give, and gives that little quietly and calmly—that man's heart is the home and resting-place of true charity, most acceptable to the throne of Heaven, valued as the "widow's mite."

SPRING IS COME AGAIN.

Birds are singing, music ringing,
  For Spring is come again!
Sweet flowers blow, oh what a show!
  For Spring is come again!

Bees are humming, insects drumming,
  Farmers sowing, cattle lowing,
Lambkins bleating, no more skating!
  For Spring is come again!

Buds are swelling, rivers welling,
  And fish dash up the streams!
Doves are billing, ever willing,
  For love's in all their dreams!
Pigeons cooing, blue-birds wooing,
  For Spring is come again!

18

The frogs at play now croak away,
  The grass is green and growing,
And every night the sparkling light
  Of fire-flies brightly glowing,
Sweet gentle rains steal o'er the plains,
  For Spring is come again!

Green trees and shrubs, and worms and grubs,
  And lovely views, and noiseless dews,
Succeed the ice and snow,
  And cocks and hens, and hills and fens,
Put forth their beauties now!
  Our spirits light, as diamonds bright
Our eyes now flash with pleasure,
  The happy smile is seen the while,
Our hearts enjoy the treasure.
  Sweetest flowers, charming bowers,
Breezes soft—all aloft,
  Clear, serene and bright,
For Spring is come again!

Sunbeams streaming, warm love teeming,
  All nature seeming—
Rich and full of light!
  For Spring is come again!

Then let us give, while yet we live,
  Our holy love to God above
And thank forever more,
  That Spring is come again!

WASHINGTON, D. C., 1852

RELIGION.

DARE I touch this holy theme? I who am regarded by so many as an infidel, an unbeliever, because I am a member of no particular church; because I am not to be seen regularly seated in holy places on holy days, exhibiting myself to the public in testimony of my religion.

Yes, I dare! and further, I dare to say that a regular and constant attendance at places of religious worship is, in my opinion, no certain evidence that the attendant is a Christian in faith or acts. Christianity is charity, love, and good-will towards our fellows; forgiveness; doing good to our neighbors; making peace; abstaining always from all acts or words that might under any circumstances insult, wound, injure, provoke, or mortify any human being—that is the religion taught by the Saviour of the world.

Should any doubt it, I refer to Christ's sermon on the Mount; there is more charity in that chapter than is necessary to convert all good men to Christianity, if they will read it understandingly with the proper spirit. That sermon embodies the whole Christian creed; it carries evidence of its purity and truth and divinity in every sentence; it is manifestly of heavenly origin.

Christianity is infinitely superior to any other religion practised or acknowledged in this wide world. I have carefully read and studied all the known written religious creeds of very many nations and people of the earth. In many of them can be found reason, charity, and morality, and forms of worship worthy the untutored children of nature; in some there is much sublimity, beauty, and pure devotion—at the head of which stands the "worshipers of the sun." There is in that religion much natural reason and truthful adoration, and if wrong almost excusable. But far, far above all preeminently rises the blessed holy Christian religion. There is no doubt of its truth and purity, its strict morality and glorious divinity.

Christ himself gave numerous and unmistakable examples and lessons of his blessed creed, and in all no evil can be found, nor has any ever been suspected, and therefore the Christian religion will ultimately triumph over all the earth.

The religion of Christ, wherever practised, in whatever land, has ever had the happiest effect on the condition of females—it raises them from the slaves to the companions, friends, and associates of man; it makes them man's equal in all the duties and enjoyments of civilized life, increasing their value and importance a thousand-fold; it gives them the rank and station in the world the Creator intended when he made

Eve the "bone and flesh" of her companion Adam. All females should be Christians in profession, practice and faith.

But building churches and regularly attending them; publicly praying, however often; exhibiting your professions to the world; throwing your man-created dogmas into your neighbors' faces; sending "unanointed and unannealed to Hades" all who will not subscribe to your doctrines; abusing other denominations for believing what you call heresies; slandering the teachers and members of other sects; denying to others (as wise as yourself) the right to judge and think for themselves—will never make you a Christian.

To be a Christian—faith, hope, love and charity—unsullied, pure and holy—must dwell in your heart.

The true Christian ever worships his God at all times and in all places; his heart is ever thankful; his gratitude is ever welling over; his soul is full of charity for all creatures; he does no evil, he thinks no evil, his sole wish is to do good, he loves his neighbor as himself, and does unto others as he would have others do to him. No envy, malice, hatred, jealously, revenge, slander, or evil towards his fellows has a home or resting-place in the heart of a Christian.

Religion is from God! from Heaven!
To mortals all 'tis freely given,
Who wish to have and truly feel it,
God knows when and how to reveal it:
His work is pure religion.

The *heart* that gives devoid of art
To all who need at least a part,
For *others'* woes can feel the smart;
The *meek,* the *kind,* the *generous heart,*
Is true religion's home!

Do good, shun vice, love God and peace;
Ask for help, and never cease
To aid the suffering sons of Heaven
In every way the power is given:
That's pure religion!

A PRAYER.

Almighty God! who governs all
The rich, the poor, the great and small;
The wise, the weak, the high and low ;
From whom our hopes and blessings flow.
God! to whom we adoration owe,
And all the good we feel and know;
Who gives us light, and strength, and wealth
Who gives us life, and food, and health;
Who shows the *way* we all should go—
Chastises those who *will not* know.
Great God, this one petition grant—
Thou knowest best what mortals want:
Oh, God! what's good wilt thou supply—
What's evil to my soul deny!

ENVY AND JEALOUSY.

Among the most degrading and contemptible passions which debase the human heart are envy and jealousy. There is an inexcusable, unpardonable meanness in envying the good fortune of a fellow-being; that a man of sense should be ashamed of, and a Christian should never permit such feelings to rest in his bosom. An honorable man will rejoice at the successes of his neighbors and acquaintances, and heartily congratulate them on all such occasions.

The envious man looks and feels degraded, for the sin is ever accompanied by falsehood, slander, and cowardice; he carries in his face and on his tongue positive evidence of his infamy, and as he looks and speaks all present know the gnawings of his polluted heart.

The dastard soul rankling with envy and jealousy finds purgatory (or worse) on earth, for the gall wells over at every good to his neighbor he hears of, and at everything good for others that he sees.

I cannot imagine a greater curse upon a human being than to fill his heart with envy and jealousy, for there is no peace for him. Should an associate speak well or kindly of any one, he hates the speaker and the one spoken of. Should one be lauded for his virtues or talents, the envious man is not only jealous of the superiority, but hates him who speaks of it. The gallant, chivalrous, heroic, and honorable deeds of others are, to the envious and jealous, eternal sources of pain.

When quite a little boy I was taken by my parents on a visit to some relations in an adjoining county, where there were several children of from two to ten years of age, and others in the immediate neighborhood of the same description. One boy, in his sixth year, had just received a large gaudily painted humming-top, which all the juveniles collected were particularly delighted with, and I perhaps as much as any other, for having never seen one before, my anxiety to try to spin or make it hum was very great and very evident; and I repeatedly begged the fortunate owner for permission to exhibit my skill, which to my deep mortification he positively refused; and to several other applicants he was equally rude and selfish. I retired a little distance and, *malgre* my pride, tears filled my eyes, which my kind and ever attentive nurse immediately noticed. She knew the cause of my distress, and while endeavoring to soothe me, an elder boy snatched the top from the cross-grained little owner, and throwing it with all his strength on the floor, broke it into a dozen pieces, which produced forthwith a grand squallification, fully equal to the finale of an Italian opera.

I was coming to my senses quite rapidly under my nurse's arguments and reasonings, and to the best of my recollection had never, until that time, heard the word "envy" used. She told me the destructive little gentleman was a very bad boy, that he envied the owner of the top, who however ill-natured and cross, had a right to the toy; and that I ought to be more of a man than to want other boys' playthings, even for a moment, when they did not wish me to have them; and that my father would get me a nice humming-top the very next time he went to town, if I would be a good boy. And that if I would lend it to my playmates cheerfully they never would break it, but play with it carefully, return it in a short time, and love me always after. That none but bad children envied others and were jealous of their playthings.

As young as I was, her pleadings carried something like conviction to my heart, and gave me an idea, if not a perfect and just conception, as she appeared to have, of *meum et tuum.* I felt myself rather degraded, but thought the boy who broke the top a perfect little savage and much worse than I was disposed to believe myself; for, although I was very anxious to have the top in my hands for a little while, I certainly had no idea whatever of destroying it because it was refused me. The smashing boy was soundly switched by his father, who a few days after sent the despoiled and selfish little scamp a new top, which was a panacea for all his wounds.

Now the words "envy and jealousy" still somewhat annoyed me, and I questioned my mother more particularly as to their meaning. When the story of the top was told at length, my nurse giving a faithful account of the transaction and of my longings and grief on the occasion; my mother explained patiently and fully the meaning and evils of envy and jealousy; made me understand why good people would never envy or be jealous of the possessions, or success, or good qualities of others.

The very next day I was blessed by my father with the ownership of such a beautiful humming-top as caused the envy and jealousy of all the little boys in the neighborhood. But I never refused it to one of them; and it was spun and hummed by us all, to the great delight of all, for many, many months; during which time I was particularly popular, and if the voices of my young companions could have made me so, I would have been at least a member of Congress.

That was another lesson in childhood which has never been forgotten; and if I know, or have known my sensations since, I do not think I have ever envied any human being, unless it may have been sometimes (when rather melancholy) the gay, careless, thoughtless, merry, musical, happy southern negro slaves—who most positively are, unquestionably and beyond all doubt, the happiest of all human beings;

whatever demagogues, fanatics, or ignoramuses may think, write, or say to the contrary. I have looked on those dark-skinned, contented, improvident, protected creatures with feelings too much like envy, and they are worthy objects. But few of them ever envy any other of God's people, and but few are ignorant of their happiness. Certain madmen or bad men have for vile purposes made slavery in the southern States a political question, hoping to ride into power on such a hobby-horse, and I know I should not mention the subject, for God knows I do not *envy* them, and shall never feel *jealous* of their notoriety.

The man who gives envy or jealousy a home in his heart, nurses a viper and feeds a cancer, to sting and gnaw to death all his hopes and prospects on earth. Man should exert all his powers of philosophy to be contented with his lot, his fate, his destiny; for in my soul I believe that the God of the Universe distributes equally, and fairly bestows a share of good on each of his creatures; and if we do not fairly enjoy it, it is our own fault, and we richly deserve any punishment thus brought on ourselves. *Qui invidet minor est.*

SUMMER.

SUMMER now with glowing heat
Is come again! in riches sweet,
Of all the beauties ripe and fair
That nature's God prepares
For all his creatures, high and low,
To use with reason here below;
Fruits so tempting, luscious, sweet,
That gods as well as man might eat.

Kind mother earth's productions rare
In great abundance ever fair,
Surround us all on every hand,
Of every kind throughout the land.
No want of bread is here yet known;
No blight attends *our* seed when sown;
For God looks down on us with love,
And sends our blessings from above.

No farmer's stalks, with haggard mien;
No struggling mortal now is seen;
Food in plenty o'er all the earth,
And *good* is thrown to all of worth;
O'er all its sons, on every hand,
Of our most favor'd, happy land.

How good is God, how great is He,
How thankful we should ever be
For all His mercies — gifts so rare;
For all His blessings, love and care.
And now let's bow to God on high;
Give glory to our God on high;
And ever with our latest sigh,
Give glory to our God on high.

DUTY OF PARENTS.

WHO but a mother can appreciate the holy sensations, the intensity of love, produced by the first cry of her infant? I have thought I could understand them, but time has convinced me their value is only known to a mother. She draws it to her bosom, forgets her pains, thanks her God for the gift, and only asks:

"Is it perfect."

It is the first or another link of the chain that binds her to her husband, but at that moment her heart throbs only for her babe. She only wishes to live that she may never part from it, but nurse and love it forever.

A mother's duties commence at the birth of her innocent child. If I am wrong, may heaven forgive me, I cannot believe that an infant comes into this world a condemned sinner; it is in direct opposition to my firm conviction of the justice of the Creator; and the babe, whose only act in this world is a cry of pain, cannot be a sinner.

A mother has no thought of her child, but for its comfort and health; she may neglect all else for a while, but her child never. She may err sometimes in her management or judgment, but generally a mother is the best and safest nurse for her child, and if it be a female, a mother is the best attendant, teacher, and friend, till it arrives at womanhood. A kind word from a mother will control, nine times out of ten, more certainly than scolding or whipping a child; that should never be resorted to until oft-repeated kindnesses has failed. An attentive and sensible mother can very soon, without severity, make her child obedient, tractable, and docile; and a mother's teaching, precept, and examples are never forgotten, and always respected and valued.

If in a mother's power (without neglecting other duties) she should be the sole instructress of her daughter, and be with her, talk freely and pleasantly with her, till fate or fortune separates them.

From the rules and necessities of civilized society, much of a father's time (or so much) cannot be given to his children as a mother's; but his duty to his children should not be neglected. Much, very much depends on his particular attention, and he should at every opportunity confer and consult in the most amicable manner with the mother, as to the best manner of treatment, best studies, best books to read, best manner of dressing, best amusements and playthings; and the temper, habits, disposition, and conduct of their children. All cannot be governed alike. Some are naturally more amiable, and some more mischievous, vicious, or unruly than others; some require very little correction, others much; parents, however painful it may be, must not forget that "the rod was made for the fool's back," and that if we "spare the rod," we may "spoil the child."

No parent should ever strike a child when in a passion; however young, the child knows when a blow is given in anger; it thinks the blow is to gratify its parent's revenge—and such a blow never corrects. The man who would double up his fist and knock his child down in anger, deserves the gallows.

Parents should never deny or studiously keep from a child any article whatever which they frequently use themselves. Children are more observant, even when very young, than most parents are willing to believe; and then curiosity and cunning are sometimes the cause of deep mortification and astonishment. Nearly all transactions and remarks are noticed and remembered by children; and words spoken jestingly are too often repeated by children, at times particularly *mal apropos.* Tittle-tattle, petty scandal, light talk of neighbors, should never be indulged in at any time, but certainly never before children; they should never hear it, for they will repeat it, and shame and bad feeling are the inevitable result. Children should have much time to run about and play in the free and pure air; confinement, under any circumstance, injures or destroys health. Too much study or confinement is worse for a child than too much liberty. Let them exercise in every way freely; it strengthens and gives elasticity to the minds and bodies of males or females. Make companions and associates of your children, set them good examples, speak to them kindly and affectionately; but chastise and correct them promptly and positively, from their infancy, on the slightest deviation from your orders, or the slightest disposition to rebel, or evidence of disobedience.

Convince them early that you must be obeyed and much future trouble will be saved. It is folly in the extreme to dress children expensively, whatever your circumstances may be. Plain, neat, and clean apparel is much better for girls and boys, and it is not only a bad example to others, but leads and tempts children to acts of dissipation and even crime. A fondness for "fine clothes," has been the source of much evil.

Daughters require peculiar attentions from their parents, from their childhood till they select a protector, (as a husband is called.) It is very important that the associates and friends of girls should be known to their parents; all depends on early impressions, if good or evil, time never entirely eradicates them; and what children learn adults remember. A child never forgets the acts, deeds, or remarks of a new companion who is a year or two older. How careful then should a parent be, in permitting strange playmates to be alone with their daughter.

Daughters are like the finest porcelain vases. The least flaw or crack in the character of a female remains forever; there is no mending it, no hiding it from public view, no securing it from the remarks of those ever fond of slander and tattle. It is the duty of parents to guard as strictly as possible, their daughter from all associates whose morality is in any way suspected. One girl of evil propensities and of careless morals can destroy a whole school; and it is my firm conviction, that a "boarding-school for young ladies and misses," is the very last place (that has any pretension to decency and respectability) that parents should ever send a daughter. If possible, a mother only should teach a daughter. Parents had better hire everything else done in a family, than pay for the board and education of a daughter away from a mother's care and watchfulness. When a daughter is the constant companion and associate of a mother, she is far removed from evil—she is sure of good advice and good examples, which will never be forgotten; and, in after life, should she unfortunately be exposed to bad examples they take no hold, make no impression, and have no evil effect. There may be some very good schools for females—I hope there are—but my very long experience justifies me in saying that, at the very best of them, girls learn more "fiddle-de-dee nonsense," frivolities, and extravagances, than useful, valuable, interesting, and necessary accomplishments. The vicissitudes of life, particularly in this country, make it absolutely necessary for all females, it matters not what station they hold in society, or how wealthy their parents may be, to learn all duties appertaining to housekeeping, and to make up their minds in case of necessity to perform them.

All intellectual and ornamental accomplishments added to those considered necessary, will surely increase the worth of the possessor, but they are secondary, and the useful should be first acquired. No mother should cook and wash who can pay for her children's education, if she can teach them herself.

She should pay for scrubbing, washing, cooking, and other labors in her family, and as a lighter and much more pleasant duty, instruct her children. I have no opinion of a mother's good sense who prefers to perform the menial duties of her household and pay for the education of her children. The mother who boasts of such onerous services, and sends at a much greater expense her children to a boarding-school, is "penny-wise and pound-foolish."

When boys arrive at the age of thirteen and fourteen, if the father's means permit, he might supply a private teacher or send them to the best public school at his command, for the morality of boys (such is the way of society) is not such brittle matter as girls, and their intercourse with the world almost makes it necessary to throw them abroad, and let them take their chance for good or evil; but the parent's advice should follow them, and when away from examples, "line upon line, and precept upon precept," from "home, sweet home," should ever attend them.

A boy is often benefited by changes in situation and condition; it enables him to contrast his early life with the present, and if he have a fair share of common sense he benefits by it and informs his parents, asking further advice. But let this be understood—parents cannot devote too much of their time to the instruction of their children; and, above all, good examples and advice with proper teachings, will do more to make them valuable, useful, and respectable members of society than all else.

MY DOG.

The lowing herd — the bleating sheep —
The warbling birds are all asleep;
My faithful dog hath softly crept
Into the box where dogs have slept.
But he remains awake to guard
The master, kitchen, house and yard.
Of all *the world,* of bond and free,
All are asleep, but the *dog* and me!
He often growls, and sometimes barks;
The thief and robber he surely marks;
The honest man he lets alone,
And wags his tail or gnaws a bone!
My dog is happier far than I!
He never heaves the heart-felt sigh;
He has a friend — a master near,
Who loves and treats him with much care;

Who sees him oft, and pats his head,
And knows he has his daily bread.
The dog is grateful, good, and true,
And dearly loves his master too.
He loves to *live*, and *eat*, and *hear;*
But *I*—a wounded, "stricken deer;"
Life's ties broken, life's charms gone—
World—I have lov'd thee—I have done!

INGRATITUDE.

Of all the crimes known and indulged in by civilized society, ingratitude only is without cause; it is unmitigated, detestable, degrading and infamous; it is of frequent occurrence; and it is without a law, ordinances, or regulation to punish it. The *ungrateful* stalks abroad fearlessly; knows and feels his obligations; meets his benefactor with averted scowl; is reminded of his debt by the glimpse askance, and wishes his friend at the bottom of the ocean, in order that a sight of him might now again put him in mind of it. The man in whose heart ingratitude dwells is worse than a viper warmed into life on your hearth, and then stings you for it.

It is the reptile's nature—it knows no friend; all animated creation is its enemy, and it bites, stings, and poisons to defend itself! Man, when he receives a favor of kindness, knows, feels, and understands it; he should never forget, but with pride and pleasure remember it forever, with heartfelt never-ending gratitude; and a disposition and determination to be equally kind and generous; not only to his benefactor but to all others in need, when it is in his power.

Many years since I was on my way north in company with one of the most wealthy men of the south, an old bachelor, and an accomplished gentleman and scholar, he had traveled much in Europe; was a keen observer, and knew his fellow-man perfectly. He related many of his adventures in such an interesting manner to me (then a young man) that they were indelibly impressed on my mind. He inherited an immense estate, was truly charitable, yet he added to his wealth annually to the end of his life.

"When," said he, "I entered college, almost

a boy, my guardian furnished me most liberally with money; it soon became known; and you have no idea of the numbers who sought my acquaintance, intimacy, and friendship; at which I was perfectly delighted, never dreaming of or even suspecting any selfishness; and I soon became decidedly the most popular young gentleman in the place—often, very often was I asked for a small loan, which was never refused, and my happiness was greatly increased by knowing that it was in my power to relieve (for the time) as I verdantly supposed so many friends. But a few months passed ere I found that some of those to whom I had loaned most kept out of my way, evidently dodging me; they had always been treated most kindly and courteously by me, and their apparent intentional avoidance mortified me; I had never thought of asking them to return the loans, for I took it for granted they would do it so soon as it were in their power. Others though soon took their places, borrowed my money, and in due time also kept out of my way. This went on for many months, until my associates in the whole school dwindled down to three—who had never borrowed a cent from me. The thing worked on my mind; I feared I had done or said something unintentionally that had pained or wounded them.

"One of them I had a sincere and warm attachment for, and his absence distressed me. I had never mentioned to any one that I had ever loaned a shilling to any one. But to C——, one of the three who were yet my associates, I mentioned the strange conduct of T. S——, when he looked keenly in my eyes and asked:

"'Have you loaned him money?'

"I hesitated, stammered, and thought it rather improper to reply, and was endeavoring to avoid it when C——, with a smile, saved me the trouble, saying:

"'I know you have—he never will return it, and you may rest assured you have lost your friend and money too; as nearly all do at college under such circumstances.'

"I was shocked, thunderstruck, and uttered the first oath in my life, by swearing that by —— I never would lend money to a friend again!

"And now," said he, "I will relate an incident which occurred twenty-five years after I left college. I was in Italy, where I had just lost an only brother; I was in bad health, melancholy, in want of companionship, congenial society, and accidently (as I thought) happened to meet in a gallery of paintings a gentleman, whose particularly genteel appearance and manners attracted my attention; he noticed my gaze and very respectfully bowed; for several successive days we met in the same way at different exhibitions or places of interest or amusement, but without interchanging a word. I was perfectly fascinated by the man's appearance; and on our next meeting I waived a formal introduction and handed him my card, which he received with the grace of a Chesterfield, and presented his in return; we entered into conversation, and I was charmed as never before!

"I mentioned that in a few days I should leave for Switzerland, where I expected to spend the summer; he very pleasantly replied that such was his intention, and asked in what part of Switzerland I would remain. I told him at or in the neighborhood of Lake Como; when he exclaimed:

"'Strange coincidence; I intend to spend the greater part of the summer there myself, and then to Paris.'

"'Exactly my route,' said I.

"'And then to London for winter,' said he.

"'And so do I,' both laughing quite heartily at the singular accordance of our views.

"We left together, were traveling in very much the same style, and most charmingly did the time pass away; my mind was relieved, my health improved. In company we reached the Lake, and there was no alloy to our enjoyments, amusements, happiness. For a short time my

21

friend left me on a trip to Berne as he said, to receive funds deposited there for him; and on his return I was again happy. Our time being out we left the land of mountains, lakes, and beauties, and together arrived at Paris. The morning after I remained in my chamber, writing letters until after noon; and was just ready to go out when my friend entered without knocking, apparently rather ruffled or agitated, saying or asking rapidly:

"'Mr. P——, have you a thousand pounds to spare a few days? Some strange neglect of my agent in not having funds deposited here for me as directed has incommoded me very unexpectedly.'

"I looked at him, remembered my college friends, and most firmly replied:

"'No sir! I love you too well to lend you money. I have sworn never again to lend money to a friend, for by —— sir, I never did do it without losing both my friend and money.'

"He bowed most gracefully, turned on his

heel, and in a most dignified manner left the room without uttering another word, and I have never seen him since; but I heard from him at London. My banker told me, that a man had been apprehended and was then in prison (for various robberies and swindling) who had followed me from Florence through Switzerland and France, to Paris, purposely fitted out and prepared to rob or swindle me, by his confederates in London (one of whom accompanied him as his servant,) who knew that I had several thousand pounds at my command on the Continent! There was an escape! And now remember, you are a young man, never lend money to a friend, for you would be certain to lose both! Never trust to appearances, for the mildest looking man I ever saw was an infamous, a notorious robber and murderer. There is an episode! It teaches what is hard to practice, but who that has lived fifty years, will not acknowledge there is too much truth in it."

Ingratitude has wounded me; has more deeply

lacerated my heart than all other evils of life that have too often fallen upon one who naturally desired to love all creation! I have seldom (particularly) benefited a human being who did not subsequently (apparently) hate me for it; hate to see me; hate to know that I lived to remind him of his obligation! This is indeed the dark side of humanity, but the side exists; would to Heaven it did not.

Christianity teaches and commands us to aid all our fellows in distress, and the ingratitude of many should not deter us from the constant practice of the virtue. All are not ungrateful; and hereafter I may give you some interesting instances, exhibiting the bright side of humanity; there are diamond spots that sparkle and illume the human heart; there are those of God's noblest work who delight to remember kindnesses, and to return them at every opportunity; there are men who ever kindly remember favors, and who never forget a friend in adversity.

JENNY LIND.

'Twas sweet to see her happy face,
 Her magic, soft blue laughing eye;
To watch her movements, all of grace,
 And charms that sometimes cause a sigh!
  And then, *oh then,* the sweetest flow,
   Of sounds e'er heard from mortal lip!
  Or breathing harps when zephyrs blow,
   Or gods from dew-drops music sip!
'Twas 'witching, rich, sublimely grand!
 'Twould silence syrens—still the lyre
Of David—tho' his master-hand
 Could touch with superhuman fire!
  Heavenly choristers—angels bright—
   Before God's holy throne of grace—
  When He desires to claim *this* light,
   Who! or *What!* will supply her place?

THOUGHTS AND FEELINGS ON A SICK BED.

To see a strong man stricken down by disease, paralyzed, enfeebled, helpless as a new-born babe! What a scene! What a theme for reflection.

For nearly twenty years almost uninterrupted health and strength has attended me through all the sorrows that have been my lot, and it bore hard on me to be prostrated by pain of body. I had almost forgotten that illness might be mine as well as other woes! It came, and for many days was I thrown on the mercy and kindness of those who live to love me! There is yet left in this cold world sympathy, and charity, and kindness, and love for the afflicted at home; and those feelings surrounded me, warmed my rapidly chilling heart, quickened my almost stagnant pulsations, and restored me again to comparative health and strength.—*Laus Deo!*

"Marriage has many pains, but celibacy has no pleasures." No man, except on a sick bed, can fairly value or appreciate the never-ending attentions, and watchfulness, and affectionate kindnesses of the partner of his joys and sorrows, the wife of his bosom. He only can witness her incessant vigils; rejoice to feel her soft hand on his fevered and aching brow; see her gentle, noiseless movements, with the ever ready cup to moisten the parched and burning lips, and the ever prepared delicate nourishment to tempt the almost lost appetite; to see her watch the time-piece, so as not to lose a minute in administering as directed the medicine of hope and life; to see her smooth the pillow and arrange the disordered bed-clothes, and watch her gentle dressings of the painful blisters.

Oh, Almighty Father! these are the endearments that make us leave this world so reluctantly! To those kind friends who, night after night, assisted and relieved my worn-down and exhausted wife, I here present the warmest and most grateful thanks of a heart that *never* forgot a kindness or a favor. May they never want such attentions; may they never know pain or sorrow, and may the gates of pleasure, plenty, and peace be ever open to them and theirs.

During my illness strange visions moved and flitted before me; ludicrous and horrid looking figures would alternately present themselves. Whether I was half-dreaming or half-delirious I know not, but there they were—immense bodies, demi-human with numerous heads, legs, and arms diseased, partly amputated, dangling, bleeding, and sore! Birds and beasts with human heads, laughing, crying, or grinning as they passed along. I thought of the only animal that laughs and cries, and the numerous ills he is heir to, and wondered at the passions, whims, and caprices he is subject to, and the impositions he submits to and delights in. And then I thought of Kossuth and liberty, and Hungarians and Irishmen, and Frenchmen and French republicanism, (whew! pooh!) and nonsense and fiddledee and humbugs; and in my unsettled mind came to the conclusion, that I would not give one dead WASHINGTON for all the living wide-mouthed, windy, blustering, speech-making, money-hunting, bewhiskered, smoking, huzzaing demagogues and interventionists in and from all Europe, and the American abolitionists to boot! And I thought that if I had any sympathy or charity to bestow, I would first of all relieve every widow and orphan, and every man, woman, and child—white and black—who wanted food, clothing, or shelter in my own dear country; and then, if a surplus remained after making entirely comfortable and happy all in this blessed Union, I might go on a crusade in foreign lands, three or four thousand miles away.

But you know all these thoughts came over me while I was *peutetre un peu derange.* Man, vain man, with all his sorrows, loves ostentatious display too much, he destroys the virtue of heaven-born charity by publishing to the world his deeds, thereby squaring his accounts as he passes through this vale of tears; "laying up" nothing to his credit in the world above. He courts, covets, advertises for, and receives his full reward here; he wishes this world only to believe him charitable; he pretends to much, and exhibits his good deeds for admiration and glorification below! He cannot deceive his God and he has his reward,—is fully compensated on earth for all his works. "In my soul I loathe all affectation."

A PENITENT'S PRAYER.

DEAR God, have mercy! pray forgive
  A sinner trodden down,
Who wishes to repent and live,
  Without from thee a frown
      The remnant of his life!

Oh pity, Great Jehovah Lord!
  Your suppliant, meek, and humble;
Oh, give him *now* one blessed word,
  For comfort in his trouble
      To end his earthly strife!

Oh give him *now,* in time of need,
  One look of kindness mighty Lord;
Relieve his sufferings *now* indeed,
  And he will praise in heart and word
      Thy wondrous goodness all his life!

CLEANLINESS AND TOBACCO.

> "EVEN from the body's purity, the mind
> Receives a secret sympathetic aid."

CLEANLINESS of person is more conducive to health than medicines or cosmetics. "Want of decency is want of sense," and no man can have proper respect for himself or his associates, who appears before them unclean or soiled in person or covering. Cleanly apparel is indispensable I admit, but the entire body should be purified first—the mouth, feet, and hands particularly require the frequent use and perfect application of nature's bounteous blessing—pure water. A decent man would never offer a soiled hand to the friendly grasp of an associate; no respectable democrat should be tempted to kick an adversary with an unwashed foot; and no gentleman should present, expose, or exhibit a foul mouth, filthy teeth, and fetid breath in any company. He who neglects his mouth, will early lose his teeth; decayed and decaying teeth operate most injuriously on the stomach, and various incurable diseases are certainly the consequences. Nothing neglected can be preserved, and teeth to be useful for any length of time require daily attention, and deserve it. I am now over sixty years of age, and have every tooth in its place—there is not a speck of decay on any one of them. I know not the sensation of toothache. My teeth are as white as when I was a boy, and I have never used tobacco in any way! That is my history and experience, and nearly all I have to boast of. Now I am not digressing, for "in spite of my teeth," I have so often heard the victims of tobacco swear they were obliged to use it to preserve their teeth, that I thought my knowledge and convictions might be of importance to those who come after me. The general use of tobacco has been a cause of astonishment and wonder to me since my childhood; for I then imbibed a prejudice against the disgusting and expensive weed; and beg leave to tell you how and when.

Several of the negroes belonging to my father, who were heads of families, lived off to themselves on the plantation, and had snug little patches of ground around their comfortable cabins or quarters, in which they cultivated vegetables, and raised poultry and a pig or two, for themselves. One of them, a favorite old woman, familiarly called by all "Gramammy," kept a cow and smoked a pipe. I often visited her and was treated to milk, pea-nuts, roasted potatoes, &c.; roamed over her little garden with her, and asked numerous questions about her "truck," as she denominated everything she cultivated — amongst which was tobacco. On one occasion she pointed out to me the disgusting and enormous worms on her tobacco plants; picked off several of them with her fingers, and crushed them with her foot, when I almost had a chill, and was, as that glorious old patriot, John Adams, once said, "in a state of quiveration." The kind old woman took me in her arms, and she was then smoking her old clay pipe. I got a smell of it, the smoke nearly stifled me, and I struggled to get down. That was the first time I ever had an idea of tobacco. Gramammy took me to a stool and sat down with me on her lap—poor old creature—not thinking her pipe annoyed me, she held and talked to me; when to her dismay I dropped into her arms insensible. She screamed, dropped her pipe, ran round to the front of her house, threw water in my face, and I recovered. But that dose needed no repetition, it cured me of tobacco for ever! For a long time I deserted the poor old woman, and she was ever after associated in my mind with tobacco worms, stinking pipes, and nauseating, suffocating smoke.

I have seldom seen a "tobacco subject" who

did not have decayed teeth, toothache, a filthy mouth, bad breath, a dirty bosom, and a very disgusting habit of spitting all around and about him, to the horror of all cleanly housewives and house-servants at least. To the best of my recollection I never did spit on a floor or carpet, clean or unclean, in my life; and I have seen talented men, who were ranked as gentlemen, spit on the walls, beds, carpets, floors, chairs, tables, or anything else in their way, rather than even turn their heads. I have seen such gentlemen go to bed with a chew of tobacco and cigar, both in their mouths, recharging repeatedly, until the room, however decent on their entrance, would not "be fit," as Mr. Webster said on a certain occasion, "for a stable." I have too often seen such exhibitions of vulgarity and indecency, and have suffered much in consequence repeatedly. I have seen such gentlemen walk into clean and handsomely furnished parlors, where ladies were waiting to receive their friends and acquaintances, with their hats on, cigars and tobacco quids in their mouths, puffing and spitting as "extensively" as if the comfort of the ladies depended on the density of smoke and quantity of saliva produced.

I have had the sickening smoke too often puffed in my face when walking in the thoroughfares of cities; and I have thought a man had just as much right to spit in my face or slap my jaws as he had to blow his tobacco smoke in my face; and I have sometimes feared that I would give *striking* evidence of my opinion on on that point, by exhibiting my skill in boxing, or pulling the proboscis of the next offender, but my extraordinary placidity of temper has thus far restrained me.

That "all men are free and equal" in this country, as Mr. Jefferson said, (except the "nagers,") I will admit; but the freedom I value is not such as would incommode, annoy, interrupt, or sicken my neighbor.

A man is "free" to burn his own house down, but he must be careful in so doing not to burn his neighbor's; and should he resolve on committing or doing a filthy and offensive deed or act, he should "tote himself," as Major Meilkie would have said, "to an extensive" distance, and be alone in his glory.

The deliberate, inveterate consumer of tobacco, has no more excuse for his excessive indulgence than has the bloated and besotted rum-sucker. The one habit is just as injurious, expensive, unnecessary, and filthy as the other, and "perhaps a leetle more so," as Bob Jones remarked about the twins.

No man can be clean or decent who uses tobacco or drinks whiskey to excess. And why there are not anti-tobacco societies, I cannot imagine. Whew! I shall have all Virginia and Maryland down upon me; *mais n'importe;* it will end in smoke, for I invented a fashion "long time ago" of escaping the dangers of "duels" with great credit.

Some years since, I examined for amusement, with a fine microscope the mouths and teeth of a number of persons, and found that none were so disgustingly filthy as those of the excessive consumers of tobacco. Animalculæ of the most horrible formation and character reveled in the gums and between the teeth; they were of the beetle tribe, celebrated for their love of filth and carrion; and I would bet an apple, that no man who could see his mouth in such a condition would ever again neglect his teeth or use tobacco. I wonder not at the detestation expressed by King James II, for the pernicious, expensive, and useless weed, for he was a decent and cleanly gentleman, who never neglected the daily ablutions to make one. He had not the fear of cold water—that belongs to the treacherous feline tribe only.

Cold water is just as valuable when applied externally as when taken internally; and rum-suckers and tobacco victims should know that fact.

Temperance in all things should be remembered and strictly practiced; it is a virtue and a command, and punishment in some form or other will certainly follow its neglect.

No decent man should chew tobacco, smoke, spit on a floor, blow his nose between his thumb and fingers, or cut his corns or toe-nails in presence of ladies, that's poz. And no decent man should go into ladies' company with dirty hands, dirty mouth, or unwashed feet, the covering of which could not prevent a knowledge of the fact; that's poz, too!

To see a *thing* in human form following a pipe or cigar about the public streets, having a densely defined line of suffocating smoke in its wake, is as offensive to decency as any other act of filthiness can be; and no man who thinks himself a gentleman (or whose mamma may happen to think so) should ever indulge in such an exhibition! As to snuff! I am *not up to snuff!* and will just say, that an old lady asked the celebrated Dr. Johnson if he thought that "taking snuff" would injure a person's brain?

"No madam," instantly replied the Doctor.

"No madam, for no person who had any brains would take snuff."

That was conclusive in my opinion, and I did not wait to hear more. I deserve a gold medal for this essay, nothing less. *Verbum sat sapiente*

PARODY ON "COULD I FIND A BONNY GLEN."

Could I find a lady fair,
Warm and kind;
Could I find a lady fair,
Warm and kind;
Whose heart was always soft,
And who would kiss me oft,
Oh! I'd love her ever more,
Warm and kind.

I'd love her evermore,
Warm and kind;
I'd love her evermore,
Warm and kind;
She should no sorrows know,
While journeying here below,
I would joys around her throw,
Warm and kind.

I would joys around her throw,
Warm and kind;
I would joys around her throw,
Warm and kind:
Oh! then in heaven we'd meet,
And seraphs would us greet
With angels' blisses sweet
Forever more.

MOUNT VERNON:

THE MECCA OF OUR UNION.

On a lovely day last summer, with nearly all that is now left me in this wide world to love, I took passage on the steamer for Mount Vernon.

As an American; a devoted friend of the Union and the Constitution, *as they are*, I had long felt it my duty to make a pilgrimage to the holy and sacred home and resting-place of the man "who was first in war, first in peace, and first in the hearts of his countrymen." The man to whom we are most indebted for "Liberty, Independence, and Happiness." The man who presided so nobly over the Convention which produced our glorious Constitution; who so warmly and strongly recommended it to, and advocated and advised its adoption by, his countrymen; who was the first President of our Republic, and whose legacy in his "Farewell Address" was and is more valuable to the whole world than the mines of Golconda, Peru, and California.

Washington was, indeed, truly a "great man;" for he was, with all his brilliant achievements, a "good man;" his eulogy is indelibly graved on the hearts and memories of his countrymen, and thousands of generations yet unborn will venerate and love, from infancy to death, the man who lived and exerted himself for the benefit of his country and the world—who never performed a selfish act, and never had a selfish thought.

No devout Mahometan ever approached the mausoleum of his prophet with purer or more sincere love and veneration than I did the hallowed spot in which so calmly lie the remains of America's boast and pride and glory—her own dearly loved Washington!

Alexander and Bonaparte were ambitious, unprincipled, and bloody warriors. They were great murderers, robbers, and ruthless, selfish conquerors! Bonaparte's successes were only used to aggrandize and exalt the members and connections of his immediate family and their satellites. Alexander was a drunken madman! Where was—where is the single good to their country, their countrymen, or the world, for all their sanguinary victories? What benefit to mankind remained or followed their murder of hundreds of thousands? What was left of all their deeds of devastation, bloodshed, and destruction, to increase the happiness of posterity?

In the year 1811, the greatest divine and orator of his day, the Rev. John M. Mason, of New York, poured forth from the pulpit, from the fullness of his heart, with the mighty

"Book of books" clasped in his hands, and his eyes upturned to heaven:

"If I would be a great man, I would not be great like Alexander of Macedon, nor Cæsar, nor that Goth, that Vandal, that modern Nebuchadnezzar, that scourge of God and man, Napoleon Bonaparte! But I would be great like 'Saul of Tarsus.'"

I forgot he was in the house of God, and expected him to close (in the simplicity of my soul) or round off his peroration with the name of "Washington" instead of "Saul;" and dared to think such a finish would have been just as rich and beautiful, and perhaps as effective.

We landed, and all struggled slowly and tiresomely up the hill; and after silently looking upon the last home of the good and great with sensations that Americans can only have, I roamed over the grounds and buildings, the once happy and lovely residence of the Father of the Union; and my heart bled at the scene, so changed, so altered; the hand of decay and ruin is upon it. The beauties are gone—the care and attention of the master are no longer there. The charms of cultivation have disappeared; the roses bloom no more. Weeds and thistles and dilapidation have triumphed, and the value of the estate now lies buried in the vault of the Hero-Chief.

This should not be. The home of Washington, the burial-place of Washington, should be the property and under the care of Washington's nation.

Permit me most respectfully, however humble and unknown I may be, to beg and entreat my countrymen all—from the frozen Lakes of the north to the deep blue Gulf of the south—from the Atlantic to the Pacific—to petition Congress, the assembled wisdom of the Union, to purchase at any price the domain of Mount Vernon, the mausoleum of Washington, the whole estate, for the nation. Count not the cost. That sacred spot should not be neglected. It should be renovated, ornamented, improved cultivated, beautified, in honor to the memory of its illustrious owner and occupant of by-gone days, whose remains peacefully slumber in its soil; who devoted much of his time to agriculture. Mount Vernon should be made a model farm for the benefit of American agriculturists.

Petition Congress to that effect. Delay not, my countrymen. Beg, beseech, entreat the government to secure that domain! Competent and qualified persons should be carefully selected to manage, superintend, and labor, regardless of their religious or political opinions. The chief and his assistants should be practical and temperate men, with salaries large enough to command the best talent necessary; the laborers should have ample wages, and none should be removed or displaced without cause. Purchase or procure every animal of value; every ornamental, beautiful or useful tree, vine, plant, shrub, flower, grain, root, or fruit—domestic, or exotic, at home or abroad, from the extremes of the earth—and have them there transplanted, cultivated, nursed, and attended to in the most most careful manner; and pairs, samples, cuttings, plantings, &c., freely distributed among all such Americans as could be relied on to propagate, increase, and multiply each and everything so procured, and raised, or reared, or cultivated, for the benefit of the whole Union. Our soil and climate are so diversified as to be congenial to the growth and production of all animals, plants, &c., from any quarter or section of the globe.

The Mount Vernon estate is of extent quite sufficient for these most valuable and important services; and, with the aid of hot-houses, green-houses, &c., all can be nursed and cultivated there, necessary to distribute in the regions best suited for the propagation of any particular plant or animal.

It is not enough for Americans to build monuments to his memory, and to name cities and towns and counties in honor of Washington. We should protect his sacred remains from surrounding neglect and desolation. The scene of his hospitality and tranquillity should belong to his nation—his people; and for regard to his virtues and worth be kept as a paradise on earth, from which to distribute all that can be found good here, and in all nations of the world, to benefit all mankind.

To benefit his fellows was the object of his existence. Let his estate, the home of his pride, be devoted to that purpose by his countrymen. Let it be purchased at any price; make it the domain of the nation—the model farm for Americans. Let not the home of our Hero and our Father fall into the hands of unprincipled gambling speculators, who would pollute the sacred soil, desecrate his burial place, and make his residence the dwelling of vagabonds and "money-changers." Secure this estate for the nation. It is a holy duty you owe the memory of the great, the good Washington.

WRITTEN IN 1851

THE GALLANT DUTCHMEN AND THE BEE:

OR THE RAKE-HANDLE CONQUEST!

Two Dutchmen once were mowing grass
While the last sad war was raging;
They both were fond of a cheerful glass,
But a fight neither wished to engage in.

They dwelt in York, quite near the lines,
And often heard the British thunders;
They sometimes saw and heard of signs,
And left their work to tell the wonders!

But one day being hard at work,
Hans stumbled on a big bee's nest;
He was toiling like a Barbary Turk,
And did not see the bees distress'd!

Hans had a *horn* slung to his belt,
  With grease and whetstone for his scythe,
In which a *Bee* his way had felt,
  But sticking fast was not o'er blithe.

At length his *wings* he found were free,
  He humm'd and drumm'd with all his might;
Hans' *horn* did sound right merrily!
  Voo-vum-voo—'twas enough to fright!

Hans heard the sound, and said to his friend,
  "I dinks dat I hears de Pritish drums!
I vites dill I *dies*, I vites to de end,
  If te tam red *goats* does dish vay kums!"

"*I too*," said Jacob—and he laid the grass low,
  The bumble-bee wriggled and twisted and voo'd;
Louder and stronger did he hum and blow—
  The horn peeled its thunder—the poor bee was glued!

Hans knew not the sound of the bees "in a horn,"
  He thought it the British conquering coming,
He thought of his hogs, his cows, and his corn,
  And he quaked at the sound of the vooing and humming.

"Jacob," said he, "I dinks dat dey kums,
Und I dinks dat I runs—so quick ash I can;
Dem tam red goats, vy, dey beats too many drums,"
"Yaw," said Jacob, "I too," and we runs like a man.

Jake took the lead, and kept rather ahead;
Hans followed in style quite close in his wake;
He thought he was getting away from his dread,
When his foot all at once struck the teeth of a rake.

The rake in the grass, lay flat on its back,
It teeth were looking up to the sun,
The handle was pointing to the back track,
And the handle first met poor Hans as he run.

As his foot struck the rake, his body passed by,
The handle mischievously flew in the air,
Struck Hans quite a blow just back of his eye,
And the *Hero* fell down on his face in despair:

Roaring out, "Misder Pritishman, I zurrender,"
"I too," said Jacob, "and you may all our dings dake,
But vid ourzelves you'll sur ly be dender;"
And they became prisone s both—to the rake.

A DUEL IN NEW ORLEANS, IN 1829.

HAVE you ever been in New Orleans? If not, you'd better go,
Its a nation of a queer place; day and night a show!
Frenchmen, Spaniards, West Indians, Creoles, Mustees,
Yankees, Kentuckians, Tennesseans, lawyers and trustees,
Clergymen, priests, friars, nuns, women of all stains;
Negroes in purple and fine linen, and slaves in rags and chains.
Ships, arks, steamboats, robbers, pirates, alligators,
Assassins, gamblers, drunkards, and cotton speculators;
Sailors, soldiers, pretty girls, and ugly fortune-tellers;
Pimps, imps, shrimps, and all sorts of dirty fellows;
White men with black wives, *et vice-versa* too.
A progeny of all colors—an infernal motley crew!
Yellow fever in February—muddy streets all the year;
Many things to hope for, and a dev'lish sight to fear!

Gold and silver bullion—United States' bank-notes,
Horse-racers, cock-fighters, and beggars without coats.
Snapping-turtles, sugar, sugar-houses, water-snakes,
Molasses, flour, whiskey, tobacco, corn and johnny-cakes,
Beef, cattle, hogs, pork, turkeys, Kentucky rifles,
Lumber, boards, apples, cotton, and many other trifles.
Butter, cneese, onions, wild beasts in wooden cages,
Barbers, waiters, draymen, with the highest sort of wages.
Now and then there are *Duels,* for very little cause,
The natives soon forget 'em—they care not much for laws.
Attendez un peu—I'll give you one instance!
A Frenchman one day was seated in a fashionable Hotel,
Reading the news, taking snuff, enjoying himself quite well;
When a Kentuckian walked in, of most gigantic growth—
Zounds! he was near the size of Erin's hill of Howth!
"Waiter!" roared he. "Sir." "Bring me, in a flirt, some cold meat;
I'm hungry as a wolf—can't wait—must have it now to eat;
Be off, Sir, like a streak of lightning."—Away the waiter went.
The Frenchman fixed his eyes upon him—then on the table leant.
The waiter soon returned—and soon a cloth was spread,
Then came ham and turkey, and a little loaf of bread.

A condiment or two, of which there was not much need.
Our hero pounced upon 'em, very quick indeed.
"Waiter," said he, "have me a steak prepared quick,
And a bowl of hot coffee—strong—don't let it be thick."
In a few minutes, the ham, the turkey, and bread were eaten!
The Frenchman rose—*bowed politely,* (*there* he could not be beaten.)
"Monsieur," said he, "pardon mais zi'l vous plait, vil you somehow,
Jus tell me, if ees your dinnaire or your breakfas vish you make now?"
"Its none o' your business," said Kentuck—the Frenchman bowed, took his chair;
The waiter returned—coffee and steak hot—looked with a stare;
Saw the ham and *dry bones*—which he cleared off in a trice,
To give a fair chance for the steak and coffee so nice.
Those went like the first—presto—when raising his head,
(He was half-horse, half-alligator fellow—earthquake bred,)
"Waiter," said Kentuck, "have you got any cold lamb?
Thunder and lightning, how hungry I am!"
"Yes sir;" and the waiter was off again in a hurry.
Our Frenchman was now in, yes, quite in a flurry!

And as the waiter came in with the lamb and more bread
He determined to know what was meant;—so without any dread
He walked up and bowed, with a smile he'd invited,
"Monsieur, excuse me, mais en verite mon curiosite is excited,
Vil you, my fren, jus please—no offence I hope you take,
Tell me vrain is your breakfas or your dinnaire vish you make?"
The Kentuckian provoked, jumps up with a roar,
And knocks the poor little Frenchman flat down on the floor,
Saying, "To hell you impudent frog-eating monkey creep!"
Then immediately commenced an attack on the sheep.
He had finished his meal, and just called for some cider,
When a challenge was handed him—he ope'd his eyes wider,
And soon made arrangements to fight on the morrow;
Then was off—a friend—pistols and bullets to borrow.
They met as agreed on, and at the first round
Our poor little Frenchman fell flat on the ground.
Mortally wounded was he and in very great grief,
When Kentuckian walked up to offer relief;
Expressed his regret at what had happened—then said:

"I would be happy to assist you in getting a-head,
Hope you're not hurt severely that you'll soon be well,
And anything I can do — or have done — you've only to tell."
"Ah, sair," said the Frenchman, "je suis mort — I cannot survive,
Mais Monsieur, I vill tank you so long as I live,
You are ver kind — dere is but von ting you can do."
"*Speak* — say, my dear sir — quick — let me know too,
When — where — how can I relieve, or some amends make."
Then he knelt down beside him, and his huge frame did shake,
Saying "God bless you — tell me quickly — of your pains I partake;"
"Vel, jus tell me if he vas ze dinnaire or breakfas you make!"

LINES

ADDRESSED TO MY OLD FRIEND GENERAL BENBURY, OF NORTH CAROLINA.

MAN was made to mourn and die!
  Till death his sorrows never end!
He *lives* in pains and woes! Oh why
  Is this his fate, my good old friend?
To you I now address my song,
To you my bosom friend so long;
Can you relieve my fever'd mind?
Oh, you have ever been most kind!
Say, why is man forever cursed?
Why is man on earth the worst
    Of all created things?
Is he—Creation's master-work—
Whether Christian, Jew, or Turk,
    Whose praise the poet sings!

Is *he* with all his wisdom poor;
Is *he* e'er full of pains and sore
Without a place of rest?
Is *he* forgot of God indeed,
Poor and friendless, e'er in need,
And suffering when at best?
Was man alone placed here to grieve?
The *beasts* are happy I believe,
They know no *pain* of *mind!*
They play and eat—they work and sleep—
They *mate* and *love*—they never weep—
They never sorrows find!
Man, poor man, was made to mourn;
His fate is hard, his heart is torn,
His feet can find no rest—
His *mind's* diseased, his sight is bad,
His *hearing's* hard—his soul is sad—
Life's *agony* at best!
If home and wife he chance to own,
And children to delight him,
There comes a fire, by tempest blown,
And all are gone to blight him!
Destroyed are children, home, and wife,
And ended all his joys of life!

Oh, why is this, my wise old friend?
Why is man's heart but made to bend,
And break forever thus?
Is man a wretch from earliest youth?
Is he devoid of worth and truth?
Is he vile in every way?
Has he no redeeming good?
Does he not deserve his food?
Oh, how is this, do tell me, pray!
I know that man is oft unkind,
I know too well he often errs,
But then his destiny is blind,
His eyes are hid by sable furs!
Is man to blame for that?
Has man the power to choose his way
While traveling here below?
Has man the power to look and say,
"Yes, this is the way I'll go?"
Can man his destiny put aside
And step around it far and wide?
Can he select his course and then
Go as he pleases, how and when?
Say, my friend, you're wise and great,
You've known the world—oh, many a year!

Do you know much of God and fate?
Do you know *what* man has to fear?
Man comes into the world a child,
With little else save strength to cry—
He nothing knows—he asks not why,
Because he cannot.—See how wild
He looks when's mother takes
Away the breast, and makes
In play an ugly face!
The infant then mistakes,
Its parent first—and quakes
With pain—begins its race!
See him grow in sorrows early,
Inch by inch, as strengthening fast—
All that he gains daily, yearly,
But adds to pains which ever last!
And now a hardy boy is found,
He looks ruddy, tough, and strong;
But he's with troubles always bound,
And woes attend him sad and long!
At school or play few joys attend—
The fellow seldom finds a friend;
The larger rogues cheat and beat him;
Passions vile possess and heat him.

Do what he can, his plans are mar'd—
(By zounds, my friend, that's devilish **hard!**)
Nor boy, nor man has e'er the power,
To hold a joy one single hour;
The pleasures ever fly away—
No joy will last one single day;
But *pains* and *sorrows* never quit ye,
They last forever and tightly fit ye
Is man to blame for all his pains?
God knows 'tis little good he gains
In this queer world.—Do all he can
He lives and dies a wretched man!
The dog is happy, has no care—
His master loves him, speaks him fair
And fondles him, then pats his head,
And *sees* he has his daily bread.
The ox is yoked and worked 'tis true,
His hide is goaded sometimes too;—
But *that* is evanescent pain;
And tho' repeated o'er again
It leaves no wound upon the heart;
It stings to death no vital part—
No soul, no spirit living ever
Is touched and made to ache forever!

The *beasts* are happy *man only grieves;*
He works and gains, and then come thieves.
When robber-man his fellow leaves
Despoiled and murdered.—Yet man believes
In this and that, or any creed,
That fools or villains hatch up;
Aye, follows, runs with rapid speed,
And shouts for doctrines humbugs patch up.
Fools follow fools; asses, asses join;
Men swallow nonsense—all sorts of things
With or without reason none decline—
All are humbugged: peasants and kings!
Man is *born* in ignorance and sin;
(The Bible plumply tells us so,)
Then why is he accountable in
Flesh or spirit—high or low?
God!—*sinful as man is*—so made him,
Just as he came upon the earth;
And yet to do *this* or *that* forbade him.
Fettered, tied him from his birth—
Gave him passions, soul, and feeling;
Makes him *long* for "*this* and *that;*"
Keeps his senses whirling, reeling,
And will not let him stop at that;

Keeps him in a sinning mood—
  Puts *temptations* in his way;
Will not let him when he would,
  Be pure and holy, night or day.
Disposes him to sin forever,
  Places before him, fair and bright,
Sweetest food; then bids him never
  Touch it tho' hunger's at its height!
Makes him feeble, weak, and bad, too;
  Calls forth all his evil passions,
And makes him feel always glad to
  Wallow in the vilest fashions!
Man's no free agent here on earth,
  His acts and deeds he can't control;
He has no power from childhood's birth,
  To rule his body or his soul,
    His passions, or his feelings!
God makes! God governs! God disposes!
  His wisdom is far above our ken.
Man *thinks*, and *sees*, and oft proposes;
  He *hears*, and *feels*, and *tastes*, and then
He speculates on "this and that;"
Will with his comrades laugh and chat,
  And wond'rous wise appear;

He never thinks he nothing knows,
And sullenly takes all the blows
From *Him* man lives to fear!
God gave us woman.—What a gift!
Earth's angels are they ever;
Man without them could make *no shift!*
Oh, woman dear and sweet forever!
But God tempts us with His treasures—
So enchanting, so bewitching—
Keeps our passions ever itching,
And *forbids* the *offered pleasures.*
Can it be a sin to eat
When hungry, day or night,
When food is lying at our feet
Most tempting to the sight?
Can it be a sin to love
An angel bright and fair;
Are *passions* given just to prove
That passion's simply *air?*
Just look and see the happy *beasts,*
The happy *birds* and *fishes,*
They know no pains—enjoy their feasts;
Indulge in all their wishes.
They *sin* not in their joyous revels,
Are threatened with no burning hell;

They have no fears of ugly devils;
  They live in peace, and then—farewell
But man, with joys fore'er in sight—
  Forever within his reach—
Is told with threats he has no right
  To touch or taste a plum or peach,
To kiss, to love, to 'joy delight,
  To think, to eat, to revel
In any of the sweets of life;
  For dare he—☞ There's the devil!
Man's appetite is ever strong,
  Rich food is ready ever,
He can't *live* without eating, long,
  And yet he must not—Oh, never!
Then why are such passions given—
  Why the eternal wish to sin?
If man *cannot* get to heaven,
  Then open hell and shove him in!
Don't tempt him every hour he lives,
  With everything that's sweet and best,
Then snatch away what heaven gives,
  Without permitting him a taste!
Food was given for all to eat—
  Woman was made for man to love;
Are passions not to be indulged

As they come from God above?
How is this, my dear old friend,
Is man thus fettered to th' end?
That God is just, and good, and great,
Is wisdom's self, all nature proves;
That nothing evil He would create,
That *His* creatures He dearly loves,
Is the general belief below.
Is that enough for man to know?
Man is given power to think—
He has an ever active mind;
He will inquire,—desire to drink
At wisdom's fount,—and knowledge find?
He wants to know more than he ought;
He wants to know God's mighty views!
He wants to know how he was brought
To life, without power to choose
From all that's lovely before him set,
To tempt—excite the feelings given.
With all his passions scalding hot,
As if by *Satan* fairly driven,
To hell he was bound full tilt,
According to the parson's lilt!
Poor *man,* he dare not turn his head
To right or left—no, never!

He fears to move, to breathe, or tread,
The devil's watching ever!
If he but think, or smell, or taste,
Or *look* on nature's beauties,
He's told he's bound to hell in haste,
Forgetting all his duties!
Why were *senses* to man given,
Why should he feel, and see, and hear,
And taste, and smell, sweet things from Heaven;
If he must do it, aye, with fear
And trembling dread eternal wrath
To follow in his gloomy path!
Why were warmest passions placed
In human hearts, so melting hot,
If t'enjoy them man's disgraced,
And doomed to boil in Pluto's pot!
Why was man thus made to mourn?
God in his own bright image made him!
Why was man to sorrow born,
With gloomy clouds fore'er to shade him?
Why did the great Almighty God
Create and animate a clod?
Make His own image bright and fair,
Then fill it with *eternal* care?
Doom him to suffer night and day,

Give him a soul and heart, and say:
"You now have mind and sense acute,
Do not make yourself a brute.
Just look on nature's beauties rare,
To *see* and smell is your full share;
Touch not, taste not, eat no part
Of all that's lovely! do not start!
Enjoyment, peace, I give to *beasts,*
For you are intellectual feasts!
You're placed *here* a time to dwell,
And if you bear probation well;
Refrain, restrain, commit no evil,
Hereafter you *may* escape the devil!
  But if you are by passion tempted,
    By lust or beauty led astray;
  Be sure you'll not be exempted
    When comes the awful judgment day!
And has the Almighty thus decreed,
Is this man's doom in fact and deed.
  Oh God, would not doom man to sin,
    To endure all the ills of life
  While here on earth, and then begin
    In death an everlasting strife!
  No—God is good, and just, and wise,

We know not His Almighty will,
It pleases Him to close our eyes,
Until He all His measures fill!
Why is it so? Oh can you tell?
My dear old friend—I wish to know
Why *Adam* rarely fought and fell,
And tumbled man in endless woe?
Why for such an offence as his
He dared no more his ugly phiz
In Eden's garden show?
For an apple simply tasting,
What a most infernal basting
Have we had below!
And lovely *Eve,* oh why was she,
(Earth's glory, joy of all the world,)
Guiled by a *serpent,* (what was he?)
And into mad'ning troubles hurl'd!
Why were sorrows entailed upon us?
Why were *serpents* given life?
Why are many creatures noxious?
Why are hatreds, wars, and strife?
Why were toads and snakes and bugs
And insects made to bite and sting;
To crawl and creep, infest our "lugs,"

And buz forever on the wing?
Malaria, poisonous vapors too,
Float o'er us ever causing death;
Disease and pains of every hue,
Attend us all while we have breath!
'Tis now near time for me to end,
This thing is getting long, my friend;
You will answer me I know.
Have I asked of you too much?
I merely want to have a touch
Of your thoughts — *above* — *below!*

☞ REPLY.

You ask me much, my worthy friend,
But having a little time to spend,
I freely give you, short and sweet,
My views and notions quite complete.
☞ There is a place of holy rest,
And suffering mortals find a cave,
Where sorrows cease — where man is blessed,
And happy in his *grave!*
We know but little here of God,
But yet enough for us to know

He is *Almighty!* man's a clod,
  A part of earth below!
Then trust and hope in *Him* on high;
  Known duties do — in mercy save
A suffering fellow struggling nigh,
  And never fear the *grave!*
Of *soul* or *spirit* what know we?
  Hereafter is above our ken!
God gives us knowledge just to see
  Enough of life, and then
'Till his last loud trump shall sound
We'll sweetly rest low in the ground!

NOTICES OF THE PRESS.

Scenes in the South, and other Miscellaneous Pieces, by the late Colonel JAMES R. CREECY.

This work is a collection of fugitive pieces, manuscript found after death in the port-folio of Col. Creecy, a gentleman well known through the South and West by his contributions to the press, and esteemed for his gallant bearing, talent, and generous disposition.

The sketches here offered by his estimable Lady are principally graphic pictures of life at the South and on the frontier, when Choctaw was almost the vernacular of the hardy pioneer, and ash-pones and tin cups the luxuries of the settler's cabin.

There is much humor in the anecdotes and adventures of the life of the author, and in the more serious miscellanies of the volume an earnest recognition of the sentiment and best refinements which should characterize society.

The contents are as varied as interesting.—Our readers will find this a racy book with which to while away a tedious hour, and is presented in most creditable style to our fellow citizens.—*National Intelligencer*.

Scenes in the South, by the late Col. JAMES R. CREECY.

This work is what it purports to be—truthful, graphic, and graceful delineations of character, as well as scenes in the South, at this time and also in its earlier settlement. Many of the sketches are racy and amusing, and profitable lessons can be gained from the moral courage and determined action of the narrator in two or three crises in which he was placed. Without pretension to rhetorical display, or elaboration of plot, it reads pleasantly to the ear, as the genuine effusions of what transpired under the author's vision, and often a participator in them.

Amid this never-ending tirade—this convulsion of slavery, abolitionism, we would kindly ask all to peruse the lively sketch entitled, "The Language and Dances of the Negro Creoles."

The descriptions of "The Catholic Burying Ground on All Saints' Day," "The Charivari in New Orleans," are all told in a fascinating manner, and the truthfulness of which will be asserted by every visitor as well as resident of the "Crescent City." "Hospitality of First Settlers," "Anecdotes of Yazoo and other countries," will excite the risibles of the gravest, and dispel a fit of ennui.

We understand this book has been published by the widow of the above-mentioned gentleman, and that already several editions have been sold in this city alone.

We can commend it as being "true to nature," and calculated to while away a pleasant hour profitably to us.—*States and Union.*

A New Southern Book.—We have received from the lady of the author a copy of "*Scenes in the South,* and other Miscellaneous Pieces," by the late Col. James R. Creecy.

This is an entertaining volume of fugitive pieces from the facile pen of a refined and intelligent author. Col. Creecy was formerly a southern planter, and previous to his death intimately associated with the leading statesmen and politicians of the country.

His lady has gathered together the literary effusions of her husband, and now offers them in a most attractive form, that does honor alike, to the author, compiler and publisher.

Thirteen hundred copies have already been disposed of among our most prominent citizens, and no doubt the balance will be in instant demand.—*Evening Star.*

www.ingramcontent.com/pod-product-compliance
Lightning Source LLC
LaVergne TN
LVHW010213110826
845151LV00004B/1075

* 9 7 8 1 4 2 5 5 2 8 5 0 8 *